URBAN ANALYSIS
FOR BRANCH LIBRARY
SYSTEM PLANNING

Contributions in Librarianship and Information Science

SERIES EDITOR: PAUL WASSERMAN

1. Urban Analysis for Branch Library System Planning
   ROBERT E. COUGHLIN, FRANÇOISE TAÏEB, AND BENJAMIN H. STEVENS

2. Frontiers in Librarianship: Proceedings of the Change Institute, 1969
   SCHOOL OF LIBRARY AND INFORMATION SERVICES, UNIVERSITY OF MARYLAND

3. Subject Retrieval in the Seventies: New Directions. An International Symposium.
   HANS (HANAN) WELLISCH AND THOMAS D. WILSON, EDITORS

CONTRIBUTIONS IN LIBRARIANSHIP
AND INFORMATION SCIENCE, NUMBER 1

URBAN ANALYSIS FOR BRANCH LIBRARY SYSTEM PLANNING

ROBERT E. COUGHLIN, FRANÇOISE TAÏEB,
AND BENJAMIN H. STEVENS
Regional Science Research Institute
Philadelphia, Pennsylvania

Foreword by
EMERSON GREENAWAY

GREENWOOD PUBLISHING COMPANY
WESTPORT, CONNECTICUT

Library of Congress Cataloging in Publication Data

Coughlin, Robert E.
 Urban analysis for branch library system planning.

 (Contributions in librarianship and information science, no. 1)
 Includes bibliographical references.
 1. Libraries--Branches, delivery stations, etc.
 2. Libraries and community. I. Taïeb, Françoise, joint author. II. Stevens, Benjamin H., joint author. III. Title. IV. Series.
 Z686.C67   027.4   71-133496
 ISBN 0-8371-5161-9

Copyright © 1972 by Robert E. Coughlin, Françoise Taïeb, and Benjamin H. Stevens

All rights reserved. No portion of this book may be reproduced, by any process or technique, without the express written consent of the authors and publisher.

Library of Congress Catalog Card Number: 71-133496

ISBN: 0-8371-5161-9

First published in 1972

Greenwood Publishing Company
A Division of Greenwood Press, Inc.
51 Riverside Avenue, Westport, Connecticut 06880

Printed in the United States of America

Designed by Peter Landa

A royalty-free license is hereby granted for reproduction of any part of this monograph for official purposes of the United States government.

CONTENTS

List of Tables	vii
List of Figures	xi
Series Preface Note	xiii
Foreword	xv
Acknowledgments	xvii
1 Introduction	3
2 Policies and Objectives of Library Systems and Community Goals	7
3 The Library System as a Whole: Determinants of System Output	20
4 Output of Individual Branches and Economies of Juxtaposition: A Preliminary Analysis	27
5 The Individual Branch: A Detailed Survey	59
6 Analysis of the Effects of Location on Library Use	101
7 Conclusions and Implications for Library System Planning	150
Index	165

LIST OF TABLES

1. Simple Correlations between Inputs and Outputs for 107 Major Library Systems — 23
2. System Measures, Free Library of Philadelphia, 1954–1965 — 30
3. Basic Data on the Branch Library System of the Free Library of Philadelphia, 1960–1961 — 40
4. Library Output and Characteristics of Residents in Nominal Service Area: Correlation Coefficients — 42
5. Correlations between Accessibility to Schools and Deviation from Expected Juvenile Circulation, for Various Measures of Proximity — 55
6. Branch Libraries, by Location and Type of Neighborhood — 61
7. Characteristics of Residents of Nominal Service Areas, 1960 — 61
8. Data on Physical Plant and Output of Branch Libraries, 1966 — 64
9. Rate of Return of Useable Questionnaires — 66
10. Age and Sex of Library Users — 71
11. Age of Library Users — 71
12. Sex of Library Users — 72
13. Occupation of Adult Library Users and of Parents of Child Library Users — 73
14. Purpose of Library Visit — 73

15.	Services Used in the Library	75
16.	Borrowing for Use Outside Library vs. Use of Assistance from Staff	75
17.	Individuals Borrowing and Seeking Assistance from Staff	77
18.	Branch Patrons' Use of Other Libraries	78
19.	Reasons for Dissatisfaction with Library Service	81
20.	Library Users Responding to Survey, by Distance	86
21.	Other Stops on Library Trip	96
22.	Radii Encompassing 80 Percent of Users for Single and Multistop Library Trips	98
23.	Means of Transportation to Libraries	98
24.	Library Users from Outside Philadelphia	98
25.	Radii of the Rings Containing Residences of Library Users	102
26.	Users per 1,000 Residents, by Branch, Age of User, and Distance from Home to Library	115
27.	Number of Book Borrowers, by Distance of Residence, Duluth Public Library System, 1933	118
28.	Base Level Use Rate, Effective Service Radius, Market Area Radius, and Decline in Use Rate per Mile	118
29.	Bookstock of Library and Occupational Level of Residents of Service Area and of Users	118
30.	Accessibility of Libraries to Schools and to Commercial Areas	132
31.	Correlations of Accessibility to Schools and Accessibility to Commercial Areas with Basic System Variables and Measures of Library Comfort	132
32.	Correlations between Accessibility and Residuals from Regressions with Bookstock and Percent Professionals in Nominal Service Area	134
33.	Penetration and Overlap of Lovett and Wadsworth Market Areas	139
34.	Adult Library Users Who Use Lovett, by Location of Residence	141
35.	Adult Library Users Who Use Nearest Library, by Location of Residence	141
36.	Penetration of Haddington Market Area by Wynnefield	141
37.	Penetration of Neighboring Service Areas by Selected Branch Libraries: Summary	145

List of Tables

38. Penetration of Neighboring Service Areas by Selected Branch Libraries: Detail — 146
39. Penetration of Neighboring Natural Market Areas by Selected Hospitals in the Cleveland Metropolitan Area — 147

LIST OF FIGURES

1. *Linkages between Library System Policies and Objectives and Community Goals* — 9
2. *Branch Libraries in the Philadelphia System* — 29
3. *Total Circulation: Region I, Northeast* — 32
4. *Total Circulation: Region II, Northwest* — 33
5. *Total Circulation: High Circulation Libraries, Northeast and Northwest* — 34
6. *Total Circulation: Region III, West Philadelphia* — 35
7. *Total Circulation: Region IV, North Philadelphia* — 36
8. *Total Circulation: Region V, South Philadelphia* — 37
9. *Circulation per Adult Resident* — 43
10. *Circulation per Child Resident* — 44
11. *Bookstock* — 46
12. *Presence of Children's Librarians* — 49
13. *Proximity to Commercial Area and to Senior High School* — 52
14. *Proximity and Size of Elementary and Junior High Schools* — 54
15. *Adult and Juvenile per Capita Circulation* — 56
16. *Location of Branch Libraries Surveyed* — 63
17. *Questionnaire Used in Branch Library Survey* — 68
18. *Users vs. Distance of Residence from Library: Richmond* — 89
19. *Users vs. Distance of Residence from Library: Columbia* — 90

List of Figures

20. Users vs. Distance of Residence from Library: Haddington — 91
21. Users vs. Distance of Residence from Library: Lovett — 92
22. Users vs. Distance of Residence from Library: Wadsworth — 93
23. Users vs. Distance of Residence from Library: Wynnefield — 94
24. Users vs. Distance of Residence from Library: Frankford — 95
25. Radius of Market Area with 80% of Users vs. Percent of Employed Adults — 105
26. Radius of Market Areas with 80% of Users vs. Annual Circulation — 106
27. Radius of Market Area with 80% of Users vs. Bookstock — 107
28. Radius of Market Area with 80% of Users vs. Average Distance to Two Nearest Libraries — 108
29. Library Users per 1,000 Residents, by Distance to Home: Children under 14 — 112
30. Library Users per 1,000 Residents, by Distance to Home: Persons 14–18 — 113
31. Library Users per 1,000 Residents, by Distance to Home: Persons over 18 — 114
32. Effective Service Radius vs. Base Level Use Rate — 121
33. Base Level Use Rate vs. Bookstock — 122
34. Base Level Use Rate vs. Percent Professionals, Managers, Officials in Service Area — 123
35. Effective Service Radius vs. Bookstock — 124
36. Effective Service Radius vs. Percent Professionals, Managers, Officials in Service Area — 125
37. Radius of Effective Service Area vs. 80% Market Area Radius — 126
38. Percent of Adult Users Who Make Shopping Stop on Library Trip — 127
39. The Concepts of Penetration and Overlap — 137
40. Possible Penetration Flows — 143
41. Service Levels of Simple Hypothetical Library Systems — 156
42. Alternate Criteria for Minimum Acceptable Service Levels — 159

SERIES PREFACE NOTE
CONTRIBUTIONS IN LIBRARIANSHIP
AND INFORMATION SCIENCE
GREENWOOD PUBLISHING COMPANY

The essential purpose and anticipated contribution of this series is to influence for the better the intellectual currents of the field. On the assumption that the level of substantive contribution available to thoughtful practitioners and to students of the field stands in need of improvement, the mission of these publications will be to elevate this standard. The expectation is that the present publication program may achieve these ends under the aegis of an energetic and ambitious publishing organization firmly committed to libraries and to the intellectual concerns of their supportive professional discipline. Every effort will be made to influence those who, individually or in combination, have the capacity to add to the ideological, theoretical, pragmatic, and problem-solving perspectives of the field, to share their insights through this open-ended series, "Contributions in Librarianship and Information Science."

The range of material covered will vary widely. Its limits are set only by the capacity of the series editor to identify and to attract those of sufficiently broad and imaginative cast of mind who will treat the many areas and issues which stand in need of thoughtful discussion, analysis and elaboration. The nature of the work published in the series will span a wide continuum. There will be monographs and advanced or upper-division texts treating subjects of significance. Collections of essays and papers upon topics that transcend the capacity of single authors will be included. Proceedings of institutes, conferences and symposia on significant issues of dynamic or topical concern will also receive hospitality in the series. Monographic reports of research, based upon individual or group efforts, on subjects in librarianship and information science will also be encouraged. The precise form and specific framework of the published titles may be expected to vary from work to work. But the primary criterion for accepting a prospective volume for inclusion shall remain focused upon whether the manuscript or the material makes a genuine contribution to the knowledge base of the field. In bringing "Contributions in Librarianship and Information Science" into being, we have attempted to inspire the very best efforts from the most thoughtful in librarianship and information science. As in all similar undertakings, the reach may exceed the grasp, but it is upon just such a shared ambitious and optimistic note between the publisher and the series editor that the present series has been conceived and brought into existence.

College Park, Maryland   PAUL WASSERMAN
March 25, 1970

FOREWORD

The Coughlin-Taïeb-Stevens study on planning for branch library service is a significant addition to the recently growing research literature relating to public library service. The detailed information presented and the framework for analyzing use patterns and formulating system plans should be of considerable value in reviewing older branches and in planning new ones.

The conclusions reached have in many cases long been suspected by library planners, and it is of great importance to have many of these conclusions substantiated. Some notions, such as location of a branch in a shopping center is a less important factor than the bookstock or economic level served, seem to be arguable. Rather I would say that there are four or five factors that are of paramount importance and that they must be considered together and not separately.

There is still much to do in the research of public libraries: the problem of the motivation, or non-motivation, of people to use library services; to find out why adults do not avail themselves of the use of libraries to a greater degree; the problems of changing communities; and the interrelationship of various types of libraries, for example, are areas needing further research.

This contribution will certainly add to the base of knowledge concerning libraries.

EMERSON GREENAWAY
5 December 1970

ACKNOWLEDGMENTS

We are deeply indebted to Emerson Greenaway, Director of the Free Library of Philadelphia, and his staff for their extensive help in providing data and insight on the operation of the library system and in reviewing drafts of this report. We are also indebted to Vartine Beberian, Edith Hallstein, Jacqueline Harmon, Anita Holschuh, Carla Rabinowitz, Katherine Seygal, and other members of the Regional Science Research Institute for their efforts.

This investigation was supported by U.S. Public Health Service Research Grant No. UI-00160 to the Regional Science Research Institute.

URBAN ANALYSIS
FOR BRANCH LIBRARY
SYSTEM PLANNING

1

INTRODUCTION

A small city may be served adequately by a single library, but a large city or metropolitan region will require a system of branch libraries—perhaps numbering fifty or even a hundred. In addition to the size and quality of each branch, the locational pattern of the system is believed to have a significant effect on library use. In fact, since no direct charge is normally made, the major cost of using a library is the cost of getting there. The locational pattern of libraries, and its accessibility characteristics, therefore, play a unique role in determining total use.

Despite the evident importance of system pattern, few studies have been made for the planning of library systems as opposed to the designing of single libraries.[1] The work that has been done tends to concentrate on problems of administration rather than on problems of system structure. Very little data exist on the people or market areas served by libraries or on the way in which library system goals are affected by alternative hierarchical organizations and locational patterns.[2]

These latter considerations are relevant to the type of decisions that must be made by library system administrators, city planners, public facility programmers, and other professionals and government officials who are concerned with the overall functioning of urban areas. Such people must decide, for example, how many libraries of each type to build, where to locate them, and when to program their construction. It is hoped that the methodology and some of the conclusions reached in this study will also be of use to those concerned with other systems of service facilities in which the demand resulting from the areal growth of the metropolis is met by the addition of one or more relatively self-sufficient, physically isolated units. Examples of such services are health centers, hospitals, schools, playgrounds, fire stations, and police stations.

The location of public facilities is important, not only because it affects the quantity of public services available and the efficiency of those services, but also because the location and timing of public facility construction affects private development decisions. The possibility of programming public facilities to influence the form of urban growth and raise the quality of urban life could elevate public facility programming beyond the level of mere coordination or engineering efficiency. Little is known, however, of the relationships involved.[3] This research on library systems provides a beginning for estimating increases in service effectiveness, which would result from better patterns of facilities. But the question of how public-facility location decisions affect private location decisions must be left for future research.

This analysis of a library system is set in a conceptual framework.[4] The construction and operation of a public facility is envisaged as contributing first to an immediate functional goal. The magnitude of this contribution varies depending on where and in what sequence this and other facilities are constructed. Two effects are distinguished—marginal contributions by successive projects of a given type and additional benefits when projects of complementary types are combined or "agglomerated." Levels of attainment of immediate and specific functional

Introduction

goals also affect levels of the more general community goals. Finally, attainment of a given level in one goal may well affect the levels achieved in other goals.

In chapter 2, an attempt is made to express systematically and conceptually the relationships between community goals, library system objectives, and the policies that might be used to meet those objectives. Although this conceptual scheme does not provide a formal framework for the empirical analysis, it does provide a setting or context.

In following chapters, data are analyzed in an effort to determine relationships that would be useful in evaluating alternative library systems or additions to a given system. The emphasis is on how immediate functional goals are affected. A major objective of the research is to develop quantitative measures of relationships which can be tested statistically. These measures are designed so that they may ultimately be used in formulating the library construction portion of municipal capital programs.

In chapter 3, the library system is viewed as a whole. Data on 107 library systems are analyzed in an attempt to determine how circulation is affected by the resources devoted to the system.

The individual branches which make up a system are the focal point of this study. In chapter 4, readily available data on branch libraries of the Free Library system of Philadelphia are analyzed to determine statistical relationships between output, the quality of the library itself, and a branch's location relative to populations of varying social characteristics, to commercial areas, and to schools.

In chapter 5, extensive data gathered from seven Philadelphia libraries are analyzed to identify types of users, kinds of use, and the areal distribution of residences of users. In chapter 6, use rates by the residential population and radii of effective service areas are identified and related to measures of the quality of the library and of the social and economic characteristics of the service area. Overlap of market areas of adjoining libraries is examined and compared with degree of overlap found in other service systems, particularly in hospital systems.

In the final chapter, the major findings of the study are reviewed and their implications for planning library systems are examined.

NOTES

1. Ralph Conant, ed., *The Public Library and the City* (Cambridge: MIT Press, 1965).
2. Leonard Grundt, "An Investigation to Determine the Most Efficient Pattern in Providing Adequate Public Library Service to All Residents of a Typical Large City" (Ph.D. diss., Rutgers University, 1964).
3. See Stuart Chapin and Shirley F. Weiss, *Factors Influencing Land Development* (Chapel Hill: Urban Studies Research Institute for Research in Social Service, University of North Carolina, 1962), and R. E. Coughlin, "Programming Public Facilities to Shape Community Growth," in U.S., Department of Agriculture, *A Place to Live, The Yearbook of Agriculture, 1963* (Washington, D.C.: Government Printing Office, 1963), pp. 460–468.
4. See Benjamin H. Stevens and Robert E. Coughlin, *Comprehensive Programming of Public Facilities: Research Plan* (Philadelphia: Regional Science Research Institute [RSRI], 1964), and Robert E. Coughlin and Benjamin H. Stevens, *Public Facility Programming and the Achievement of Development Goals* (Philadelphia: RSRI, 1964).

2

POLICIES AND OBJECTIVES OF LIBRARY SYSTEMS AND COMMUNITY GOALS [1]

The rationale for investing in a particular public facility can be judged only in relation to the public goals or public purposes for which the facility is created. Therefore, in this chapter, the particular goals or objectives that a library system serves, the particular types of policies that affect the degree of achievement of each of those objectives, and the general societal goals or ideals that are served in fulfilling the particular objectives are identified. This policy–objective–goal structure is explored at the conceptual level only. The purpose is to provide a logical setting for the empirical studies of succeeding chapters.

A set of policies results in various levels of achievement of one or more objectives, which in turn result in various levels of attainment of one or more general goals. General goals are desired in and of themselves; objectives and policies are important primarily in their contributions to such goals. The ability to achieve goals, of course, is limited by such constraints on the system as the amount of money available and the actions which are feasible from a physical, administrative, or political point of view.

A particular policy will have an effect on some, but not all, library system objectives. In turn, progress toward a particular library system objective will have an effect on the attainment of some, but not all, community goals. Figure 1 suggests some of the major linkages that might be expected between particular policies, objectives, and goals. For example, a particular policy concerning the number of branch libraries in the system would have a major effect on attainment of the system objective of increasing the number of individuals who use the library system. Increase in attainment of this system objective would have major effects on general community goals such as increased equality of opportunity and cultural integration. It would have significant but less pronounced effects on general community goals, such as increased education, creativity, and level of happiness. The particular system policy concerning the number of branch libraries would also have a major effect on the system objective of increase in the number of books read and minor effects on the system objectives of increase in adult education and increase in juvenile education. These effects on attainment of system objectives, in turn, would have effects on the attainment of several general community goals.

The system policies and objectives and community goals listed in Figure 1 are drawn from analysis of library studies and discussions with library officials.[2] Although it consists of nineteen system policies, ten system objectives, and eight general community goals, the statement presented in Figure 1 is not complete.

The various objectives of public libraries do not affect all groups of the population uniformly. Therefore, a complete statement would require the addition of dimensions to each of

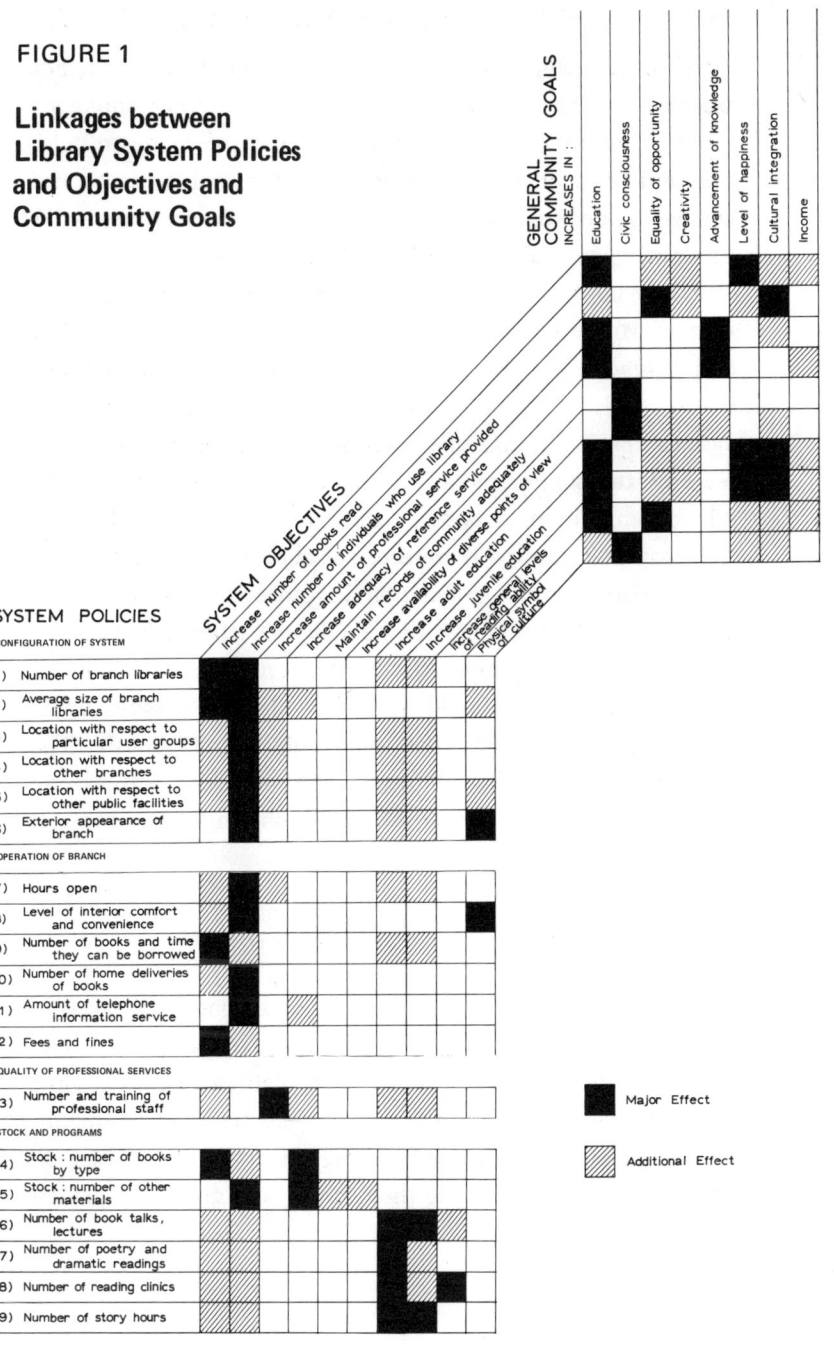

the objectives which would define the subgroups affected. For example, a simplified statement of community policy might be expressed in terms of concern for the welfare of young and old, poor and not-poor. If such a view is accepted, each objective and goal would be broken down into its effects on four groups: poor children, poor adults, not-poor children, not-poor adults.

It may be necessary to identify several additional characteristics of various population subgroups in order to trace the effect of a change in a system policy on attainment of a system objective or goal. For example, the response of not-poor adults to various library offerings may depend not only upon the income level of the subgroup, but also upon the educational levels, ethnic composition, or occupational categories of this subgroup.

It may be necessary, therefore, to examine a large number of characteristics of the population in order to predict the use which would be made of a new facility or activity. For ease in arriving at a final policy decision, however, the statements of objectives and goals should be kept as short as possible while describing the desires of the community unambiguously. The reader should keep these limitations in mind in the following discussion of the system policies, system objectives, and community goals.

LIBRARY SYSTEM POLICIES

The system policies listed in Figure 1 are those that are controlled by the library system itself. They are subdivided into four categories for convenience: those policies concerning the physical configuration of the system (the traditional physical-planning policies), those concerning the operation of each library unit, those concerning the quantity and quality of profes-

Policies and Objectives of Library Systems

sional staff, and those concerning the number and type of materials and programs provided.

Changes in policies such as these can be described quantitatively. For example, a library system can be designed by setting a number of policies, such as a specified number of branch libraries, the location of each branch, the hours each unit is open, the quality of its professional staff, and the number of books of various types in each library.

A wide variety of policies for other public service systems might influence the attainment of library system objectives. Obvious examples are school policies.

LIBRARY SYSTEM OBJECTIVES

The objectives of a library system listed in the middle section of Figure 1 are based on the writings of a number of library authorities and on discussions with library officials. Although other objectives might have been included, the objectives listed represent a rather broad view of the functions of a library system. For example, objectives 5 and 10 imply functions that might be considered relatively unimportant by many librarians. A more explicit statement of each objective and suggestions for possible measures of its attainment follow.[3]

Increase Number of Books Read
This refers both to borrowing for use outside the library building (circulation) and to consultation on the premises. It appears to be one of the most obvious and widely held objectives. The purposes for which the books are read are not specified here; they may include recreation, self- or civic-advancement, and so on. In this formulation, such purposes of library use are treated

at the level of general community goals. To make the analytic system operational, however, it would be necessary to identify reading by purpose and to determine relationships between the system objective of increasing the number of books read and the general community goals to which each reading purpose contributes.

SUGGESTED MEASURE Number of documents circulated plus number of documents consulted in the library. The first statistic is readily available in most libraries; the second might require special survey, especially in those libraries where open shelves are dominant. The objective and its measurement could be disaggregated to specify fiction, reference, and other nonfiction works. The definition could be broadened to include records, tapes, prints, films, and other materials.

Increase the Number of Individuals
Who Use the Library

The emphasis is on increasing the total number of individuals in the community who benefit directly from library services.

SUGGESTED MEASURE Number of individuals registered in library system. Number of individuals who actually borrow books during a given time would be a better measure of how widespread is the use of library services, but would be more difficult to obtain.

Increase Number of Professional Services
Provided to Library Users

The advice and direction of a professional librarian should lead to more effective use of library materials. Professional service provided is at least partially substitutable for the number of books read. Therefore, it is necessary to express the level of each.

SUGGESTED MEASURE The number of professional services per-

Policies and Objectives of Library Systems 13

formed. Where an adequate output cannot be obtained, the number of professional librarians on the staff (which is a measure of input) might provide some measure of professional services.

Increase Adequacy of Reference Collection
It is assumed that the usefulness of the reference collection is increased by the scope of the materials.
SUGGESTED MEASURE   Probability of being able to answer a reference inquiry. A more readily quantifiable measure would be the number of reference volumes found in the library as a percentage of an approved list of such volumes advocated by the American Library Association or some other professional group.

Maintain Records of Community Adequately
Systematic collection of all published material including data, journals, reports of activities, and deliberations and decisions of all local organized groups which have some significance to the community.
SUGGESTED MEASURE   Proportion of all local publications which are kept in the library. Note that it would be very difficult to make this measurement, since a comprehensive list of local publications is not normally available. In fact, the most comprehensive list and collection of local publications is likely to be that of the library itself.

Increase Availability of Materials Representing
Diverse Points of View on Social Issues
The success of democracy requires that all points of view be heard so that the good that is in each can be judged by as many people as possible.

14   Urban Analysis for Branch Library System Planning

SUGGESTED MEASURE   Probability of filling a request for a publication. Note that requests would be likely to come in proportion to the number of persons who hold a particular view. Thus, a good collection would represent all minority viewpoints, but still would be weighted toward that of the majority.

Increase Formal Adult Education
Adult education consists of classes, discussion groups, and other organized activities designed to provide opportunities for continuing education for adults.
SUGGESTED MEASURE   Number of people attending adult education activities in the library.[4]

Increase Formal Juvenile Education
Juvenile education consists of story hours, discussion groups, and other organized activities designed to provide opportunities for supplementing the programs of the public schools in the community.
SUGGESTED MEASURE   Number of children attending juvenile education activities.

Increase General Levels of Reading Ability
Consists of classes to teach people to read or to improve their reading skill.
SUGGESTED MEASURE   Number of people who attend literacy or reading-skill classes relative to existing need for such classes.

Provide a Physical Symbol of the Importance of Culture to Society
This objective refers to the role which civic design can play in transmitting cultural values of the community.
SUGGESTED MEASURE   The impact of the library building as a

Policies and Objectives of Library Systems

cultural symbol might be judged by a panel of experts or determined through an attitude survey of the citizens of the community.

The type of measurement which is feasible differs for the various system objectives listed. Three considerations are of importance: (1) the type of measure—whether it is a measure of output of the system or whether it is possible only to measure an input as a proxy for the output, (2) the scale—whether a metric scale is possible or whether only a ranking is possible, and (3) the availability of data—whether such measures are normally collected, or whether special surveys would be necessary.

GENERAL COMMUNITY GOALS

The general community goals relevant for libraries, which are listed in Figure 1, are based primarily on the following statement of library system objectives taken from a 1943 publication of the American Library Association, *Post-War Standards for Public Libraries*.[5] Words in parentheses were added and are the titles of community goals in Figure 1.

The objectives of the public library should be to assemble and preserve books and materials in organized collections and through stimulation and guidance to promote their use, to the end that children, young people, men, and women may have opportunity and encouragement:

To *educate* themselves continuously. (Education)

To keep abreast of progress in the sciences and other fields of knowledge. (Education; Income)

To maintain the precious heritage of freedom of expression and a constructively critical attitude toward all public issues. (Civic Consciousness)

To improve their ability to participate usefully in activities in which they are involved as citizens of the United States and of the world. (Civic Consciousness)

To *equip themselves* and to keep themselves equipped for *efficient activity* in useful activities and practical affairs. (Equality of Opportunity; Income)

To improve their capacity for appreciation and production in cultural fields. (Creativity)

To aid in the *advancement of knowledge*. (Advancement of Knowledge)

To make such use of *leisure time* as will promote personal *happiness* and *social well-being*. (Level of Happiness; Cultural Integration)

It is clear that the library system is only one of several institutions that contribute to any of the general community goals. There is no single goal to which it contributes the major part. Although the general goal of education (including both enlightenment and material development) may be a primary one for the library system, the school system makes a far larger contribution to this goal. In addition, the majority of book distribution is accounted for, not by public libraries or any other governmental agency, but by private purchases. In 1950 public libraries accounted for 14.8 percent of all expenditures for books in the United States; in 1960 they accounted for 18.0 percent. Although the role of the public library appears to be growing, it still accounts for less than one-fifth of all expenditures on books.[6] Because more than one person reads a library book, the expenditure figure reflects considerably more than one-fifth of the number of books read by the total population.

The community has many other goals, including the reduction of congestion, the reduction of pollution levels, and the reduction in fire losses. These are not listed in Figure 1 since their relationships to the provision of library services are rather tenuous.

POLICIES, OBJECTIVES, AND GOALS

Relationships between particular system policies and particular system objectives, and the relationships of these in turn to particular community goals are diagramed in Figure 1. Although major and minor linkages are indicated, the diagram is not based on analysis of empirical data. Rather, it is a conceptual framework within which research might be carried out on the functional relationships between library policies, objectives, and community goals.

Empirical investigations in chapters 4 and 5 are focused on policies concerning the physical configuration of the system and, to a lesser extent, on the quality of professional services and of the stock of materials and programs provided. Locational decisions (system policies 1–5) are shown in Figure 1 as having their most direct effect on the system objective of increasing the number of individuals who use the library. This system objective, in turn, affects the achievement of the general community goals of equality of opportunity and cultural integration. The extent to which the location of a new library will ultimately affect achievement of these general community goals depends upon the socioeconomic characteristics of the community in which it is located. An increase in the number of individuals who use the library would also, of course, cause greater attainment of community goals of education and income and, hopefully, of creativity and happiness. Secondary effects of locational policy decisions might include an increase in the number of books read and, because of increased accessibility, an increase in the amount of professional services used. Improved accessibility might also increase the use of adult and juvenile programs, thereby furthering the system objective of increasing adult and juvenile education.

Decisions on the size, appearance, and location of libraries can also further the system objective of providing physical symbols of the importance of culture to society. Display of such symbols can lead to enhanced consciousness of the community's pride in intellectual values. The physical symbol can also, of course, lead to increased use of the library itself, thereby raising the level of achievement of several system objectives. A more comprehensive diagram than Figure 1 would make explicit such interrelationships between goals, objectives, and policies.

A more complete analysis would also consider the effect of policies and objectives of other public agencies and would take into account interactions among general goals not affected directly by the library system itself. The purpose here, however, is to provide a simplified framework for the research of the following chapters, rather than to develop and implement a complete conceptual framework.[7]

NOTES

1. This chapter was written with the help of Morris Hill.

2. This formulation follows closely that made by Hill in his analysis of transportation proposals. Morris Hill, "A Method for Evaluating Alternative Proposals: The Goals-Achievement Matrix Applied to Transportation Plans" (Ph.D. diss., University of Pennsylvania, 1966).

3. Note that these measures are made on individual libraries and then are to be summed over all libraries to obtain the level of attainment for the system. Note further that some of the measures could probably be put in more specific form such as "per capita of poor population" as suggested in the text.

4. It is evident that this goal and three that follow make sense only relative to need. To a lesser extent, it is true that all goals are relative to need and services provided by other institutions. Establish-

ment of need on some objective basis is necessary before different libraries can be compared in relation to these goals.

5. Recent revisions of this publication have resulted in only minor changes in stated objectives.

6. Philip H. Ennis, "The Library Consumer," in Ralph W. Conant, ed., *The Library and the City* (Cambridge: MIT Press, 1965), p. 17.

7. A general framework for such an analysis is given in Robert E. Coughlin and Benjamin H. Stevens, *Public Facility Programming and the Achievement of Development Goals* (Philadelphia: RSRI, 1964).

3

THE LIBRARY SYSTEM AS A WHOLE: DETERMINANTS OF SYSTEM OUTPUT

The conceptualization outlined in chapter 2 provides a guide for tracing the effects of a specific set of policies in particular libraries on system objectives and community goals. In this chapter, however, the focus is on the system as a whole, without regard to variations in the individual libraries which comprise it. Data from a large number of library systems are analyzed in order to determine simple relationships between resources committed to the library system and the product, or output, of the system.

OUTPUT OF A LIBRARY

Of the objectives listed in Figure 1, the most generally accepted are to increase the number of books read, to increase the number of individuals who use the library, and to increase the amount of professional service provided by the library.

Circulation, a generally available and relatively reliable statistic, provides a good measure of the services actually rendered

The Library System as a Whole

by the library. The number of books circulated, however, does not give any idea of the quality of books circulated or even of what percentage of books circulated are actually read; furthermore, it does not provide a direct measure of the services a person enjoys while in the library.

Registration is a widely used statistic which gives an indication of the total number of people in an area who use library services. Although registration is correlated closely with circulation, the use that the average registered person makes of the library may be significantly different from one branch to another. In addition, registration at any given branch may not be an adequate measure of the actual number of registered people within the branch service area. The Philadelphia system is an example. This inconsistency exists because many people move during the registration period of three years and because, once registered, a person can use any branch in the system. Analysis shows that in some branches the number of children registered exceeded the United States Bureau of the Census estimate of the number of children residing within the service area of the library during the same year.[1]

An adequate count of professional services would provide an accurate measure of services enjoyed while in the library. However, where professional services are reported, as in the Philadelphia Free Library system, the reports do not appear to be reliable. A possible substitute for a count of professional services is one of professional personnel. The chief virtue of this measure would be ready availability.

On balance, circulation appears to be the most adequate and reliable measure of library service. Unlike registration, it is clearly a measure of the actual activity level in the library. Its measurement is simple and likely to be uniform among libraries.[2] Furthermore, since circulation is strongly correlated with registration and fairly well correlated with professional services, a change in circulation can be assumed to be accompanied by changes in both registration and professional services.[3]

DETERMINANTS OF SYSTEM OUTPUT

Presumably the output of a library system will be affected by the resources devoted to that system, including the number of branches, the number and quality of personnel, the types and number of special services, the level of administrative efficiency, the total expenditures, and other variables listed under system policies in Figure 1. Output is also affected by the environment within which the library system operates, including the cultural traits, educational levels, age distribution, and other attributes which affect people's desire to read; and the availability of public transportation, the proximity of the libraries to commercial areas and other public facilities.

The analysis in succeeding chapters of this report will be concerned with the individual libraries that make up a system. In this section, however, the library system as a whole will be investigated. Data are available on public library systems in *Statistics of Public Libraries (Part 1)—1962*, a publication of the U.S. Department of Health, Education, and Welfare. These data include several measures which might be considered inputs to the library system—the number of professional positions filled, the number of volumes in the collection, the number of volumes added during the year, and total operating expenditures. They also include such measures of output as total circulation, adult circulation, and juvenile circulation.

The intercorrelations of these measures for all library systems serving more than 100,000 persons in the states which comprise "megalopolis" and the "manufacturing belt" are given in Table 1.[4]

TABLE 1

Simple Correlations between Inputs and Outputs for 107 Major Library Systems

	Measures of Input				Measures of Output		
	1 Professional Positions Filled	2 Volumes in Collection	3 Volumes Added during Year	4 Operating Expenses	5 Total Circulation	6 Adult Circulation	7 Juvenile Circulation
Measures of Input							
1 Professional Positions Filled	1	0.8576	0.9133	0.4608	0.8737	0.6392	0.2689
2 Volumes in Collection	0.8576	1	0.7892	0.4836	0.7417	0.6163	0.2694
3 Volumes Added during Year	0.9133	0.7892	1	0.4569	0.9147	0.6779	0.3128
4 Operating Expenses	0.4608	0.4836	0.4569	1	0.3663	0.2724	-0.0219
Measures of Output							
5 Total Circulation	0.8737	0.7417	0.9147	0.3663	1	0.5723	0.1790
6 Adult Circulation	0.6392	0.6163	0.6779	0.2724	0.5723	1	0.2732
7 Juvenile Circulation	0.2689	0.2694	0.3128	-0.0219	0.1790	0.2732	1

Note: Statistically significant correlations (at 0.01 level) are underscored.

The results (Table 1) indicate a very high level of correlation between all variables except juvenile circulation. The table can be divided into three sectors. The upper left corner shows correlations between various measures of input; the lower right corner shows correlations between various measures of output; and the combination upper right and lower left corners show correlations between measures of input and measures of output.

Every input measure is correlated significantly with every other input measure. The correlations among total volumes, volumes added, and professional positions filled are so high that the three measures must be considered nearly equivalent. The highest correlation is between number of professional positions and number of new volumes added during the year.

Volumes added during the year and the number of professional positions filled also have extremely high correlations with total circulation, the most general measure of output. The number of volumes in the collection is also highly correlated with total circulation.

Operating expenses show a relatively low, though significant, correlation with total circulation and are not significantly correlated with adult or juvenile circulation. Operating expenses also show a relatively low correlation with the other input measures.

Juvenile circulation is not significantly correlated with any of the input measures. In fact, it shows a negative (but not statistically significant) relationship to operating expenses. It is not even correlated significantly with the other components of circulation—total circulation and adult circulation. This may be due to inadequacies in the data rather than to the actual characteristics of juvenile circulation. It is pointed out in *Statistics of Public Libraries* that adult and juvenile circulation do not always add to total circulation "because circulation systems do not per-

The Library System as a Whole 25

mit the identification of loaned material as 'Adult' and 'Juvenile.'" In addition, juvenile circulation may be different in kind from adult circulation since school homework requirements make juvenile demand less discretionary and therefore cause it to be less affected by the quality of library services.

In summary, the correlations of Table 1 indicate that the volumes added during the year and the number of professional positions held during the year are highly intercorrelated, and they provide a high degree of statistical explanation of total circulation and a lesser degree of explanation of adult circulation. Number of volumes in the collection and number of professional positions filled are only slightly less intercorrelated. Number of volumes provides a weaker, but still highly significant, explanation of total circulation.

One should be cautious about assuming any causality within the significant statistical relationships observed. Although one would expect causal relationships between the input and output variables of Table 1, one would not expect any causal relationship between number of people served and level of library service. Nevertheless, population served is very highly correlated with the number of professional positions filled ($r = 0.909$), with the volumes added during the year ($r = 0.925$) and with total circulation ($r = 0.775$).

In this analysis, library service has been viewed as a production function: if certain inputs, such as number of volumes, are increased, the result will be an increase in output, as measured, for example, by circulation. Although this view appears compatible with the data available, it is likely that the underlying causal mechanism is actually that of a demand function. Certain groups, or neighborhoods, demand more library service; the library system provides that service, that is, increases the number of volumes; and output of the library system increases, that is, circulation increases. The library system simply acts to meet the expressed desires of its users, rather than to maximize community objectives as described in Figure 1.

Left unanswered is the question of whether the library, by providing improved services to groups or neighborhoods which have not expressed a strong desire for library service, can induce an increase in library use. This question persists throughout the analysis presented in the following chapters.[5]

NOTES

1. Although number of registrants has shortcomings as a measure of library output, it may provide a useful measure of the client population served by a library system. If registration figures can be obtained by age, race, and sex, they could be compared with census figures to determine which client groups are served most intensively by the library system.

2. It may, however, be affected by the number of books an individual is permitted to borrow at one time.

3. This assumption is further supported by the results of the survey of seven Philadelphia libraries. See chapter 5.

4. Connecticut, Illinois, Indiana, Maryland, Massachusetts, Michigan, New Jersey, New York, North Carolina, Ohio, Pennsylvania, and Virginia.

5. This and other questions are also explored in David W. Lyon, *A Cost Analysis of the Oakland, California Branch Library System* (Berkeley: Department of City and Regional Planning, University of California, Berkeley, 1968).

4

OUTPUT OF INDIVIDUAL BRANCHES AND ECONOMIES OF JUXTAPOSITION: A PRELIMINARY ANALYSIS

The analysis in chapter 3 relates solely to overall system measures, which are of obvious interest. But the library system planner is concerned with goals of particular communities served by the systems and with the effects that variations in the number, locational pattern, and facilities of a set of branch libraries may have on the achievements of these community goals. Differences in neighborhoods and types of individuals served, the relative needs of these individuals for education and improvement of employment skills, and the lack of cultural integration from which some population groups may suffer, lead to a natural concentration on system objectives which may be influenced by the individual units of the system.

The emphasis in the remainder of the analysis, therefore, is on measures of the output of the individual branch and how they may be affected by various policy decisions. In this chapter, regularly collected data from the Philadelphia Free Library system are analyzed. In the next chapter, the results of a special survey are reported. Although the data are all from one library system in a large city, the results of the analysis should be applicable to library systems in other cities, since the analysis is statistical rather than merely descriptive and since there is no reason to believe that the Philadelphia system functions in a unique manner.

THE FREE LIBRARY SYSTEM OF THE CITY OF PHILADELPHIA

The Free Library of Philadelphia operates one of the largest public library systems in the country. It consists of a main library, some forty branch libraries, several special purpose libraries (such as a library for the blind and a mercantile library), and, as of 1963, the first of several regional libraries. The branch libraries, which are the main subject of this study, are mapped in Figure 2 as of 1961.

Statistics for the Philadelphia system as a whole indicate a steady growth in circulation, registration, and bookstock over the past ten years (Table 2). Per capita estimates also show a steady increase. In fact, this increase may be understated because the population estimates for 1961–1965 are probably high. The increases in circulation and registration are remarkable, since population growth over the last ten years was marked by a significant increase in the number of blacks of relatively low educational levels, who might not be expected to use libraries heavily.

Circulation of the branches as a group (exclusive of the central and regional libraries) also increased during the period, but during the last few years has leveled off. The opening of the first regional library, the Northeast, in 1963, has undoubt-

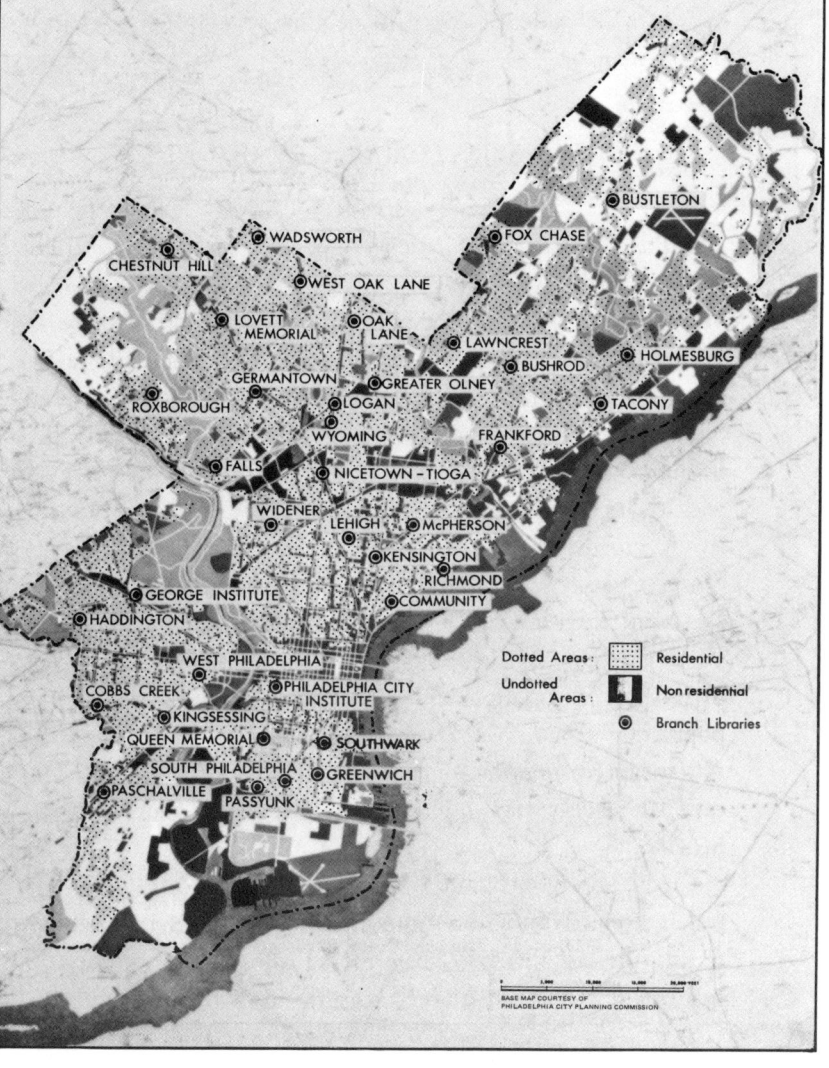

TABL

System Measures, Free Libra
(in thou

System Totals	1954	1955	1956	1957
Circulation				
Adult	2,324	2,325	2,487	2,851
Juvenile	1,942	1,751	1,877	2,176
Total	4,266	4,075	4,364	5,027
Per capita	2.09	2.00	2.15	2.49
Registration				
Adult	163	182	209	223
Juvenile	137	144	161	164
Total	300	326	370	387
Registered population (in percent)	14.7	16.0	18.3	19.2
Bookstock				
Adult	1,394	1,394	1,126	1,209
Juvenile	363	363	417	455
Total	1,757	1,757	1,543	1,664
Operating expenditures (in thousands of dollars)				
From city budget	2,593	2,647	2,851	3,361
Circulation for branches only				
Total	3,130	2,851	3,039	3,623
Per capita	1.53	1.40	1.50	1.79

Notes: Adults are all persons more than fourteen years old; juveniles are all yc
Circulation figures refer to number of books borrowed on adult and juvenile car
Population estimates of 1950 and 1960 are from U.S., Department of Commerce,
Population), adjusted to eliminate crews of vessels on the river. The estimate of 196
(April 1966). Other dates were estimated by straight-line interpolation.
Data do not include Northeast Regional Library, which was opened in 1963.

elphia, 1954-1965

1959	1960	1961	1962	1963	1964	1965
3,342	3,447	3,447	3,610	3,624	3,903	3,958
2,582	2,647	2,483	2,591	2,674	2,813	2,707
5,924	6,094	5,930	6,201	6,299	6,716	6,665
2.95	3.05	2.95	3.06	3.10	3.28	3.24
251	257	269	281	293	311	331
171	173	175	179	190	200	203
421	430	444	460	483	511	533
21.0	21.5	22.1	22.7	23.7	25.0	25.9
1,383	1,458	1,549	1,637	1,705	1,727	1,769
532	574	620	672	701	697	684
1,916	2,031	2,177	2,369	2,405	2,424	2,452
3,524	3,849	4,174	4,567	4,752	5,275	5,447
4,305	4,395	4,234	4,439	4,452	4,218	4,149
2.15	2.20	2.11	2.19	2.19	2.06	2.02

s.
type of books borrowed.
e Census, United States Census of Population (hereafter cited as U.S. Census of
adelphia City Planning Commission, Population Estimate as of July 1, 1964

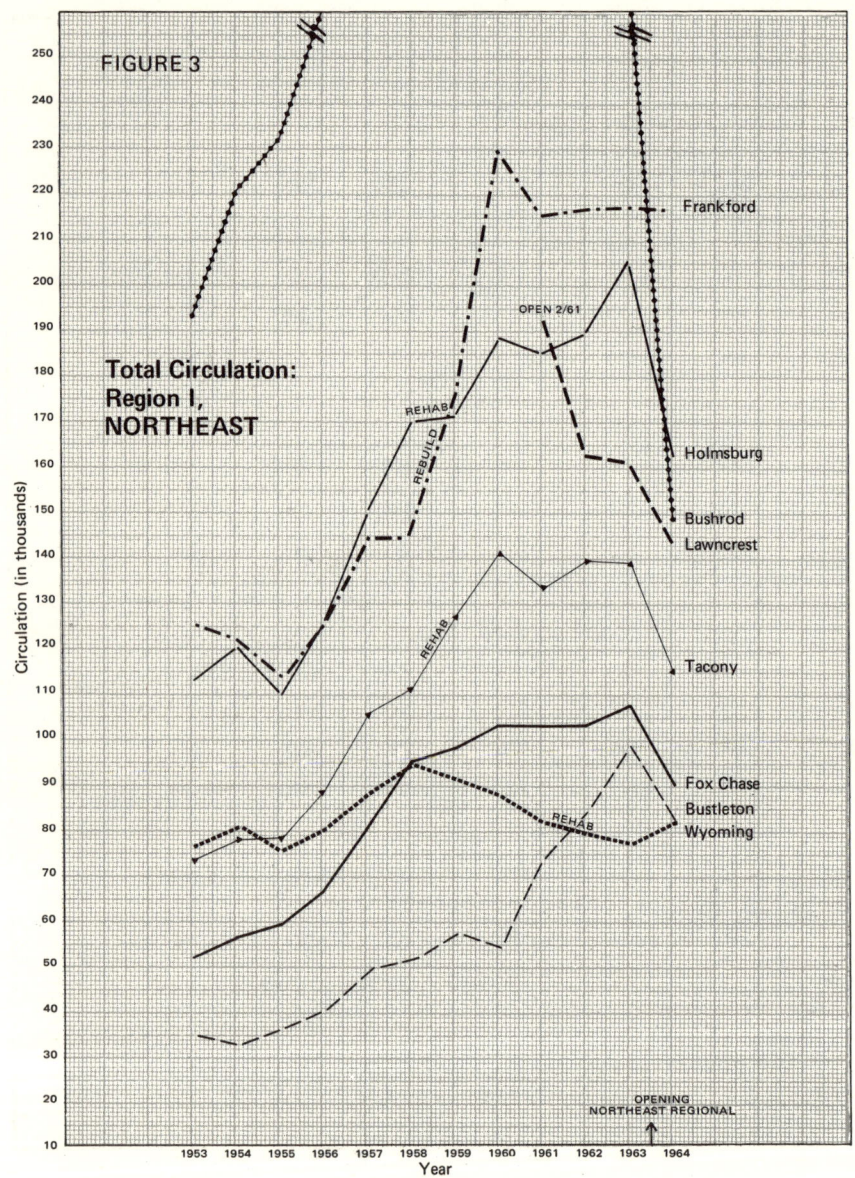

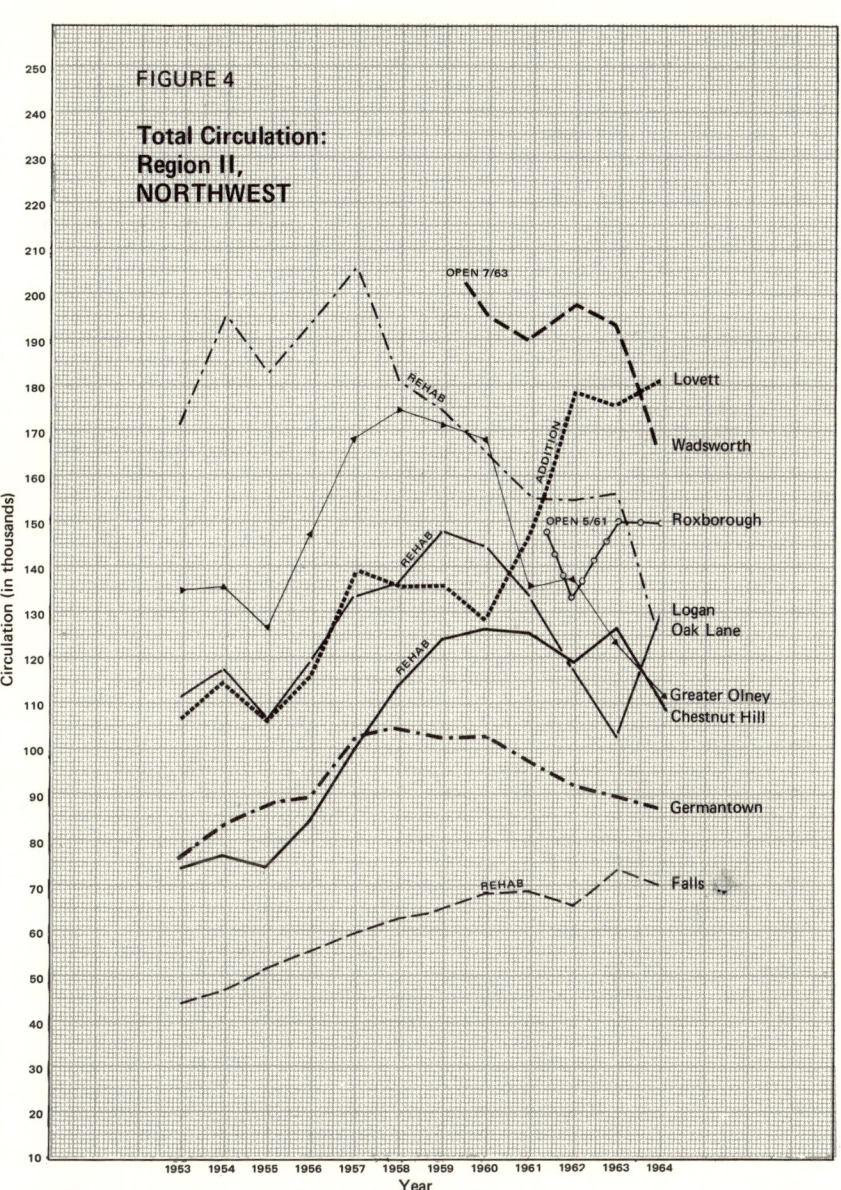

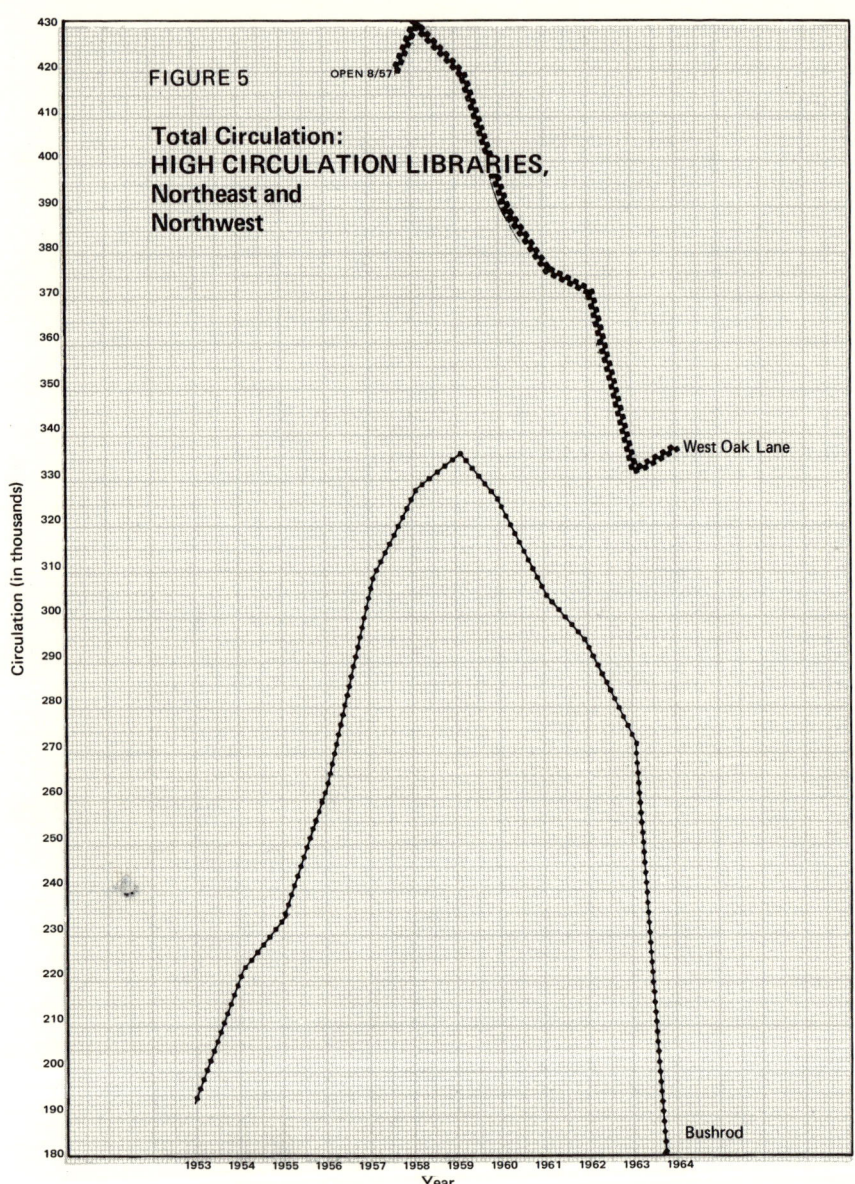

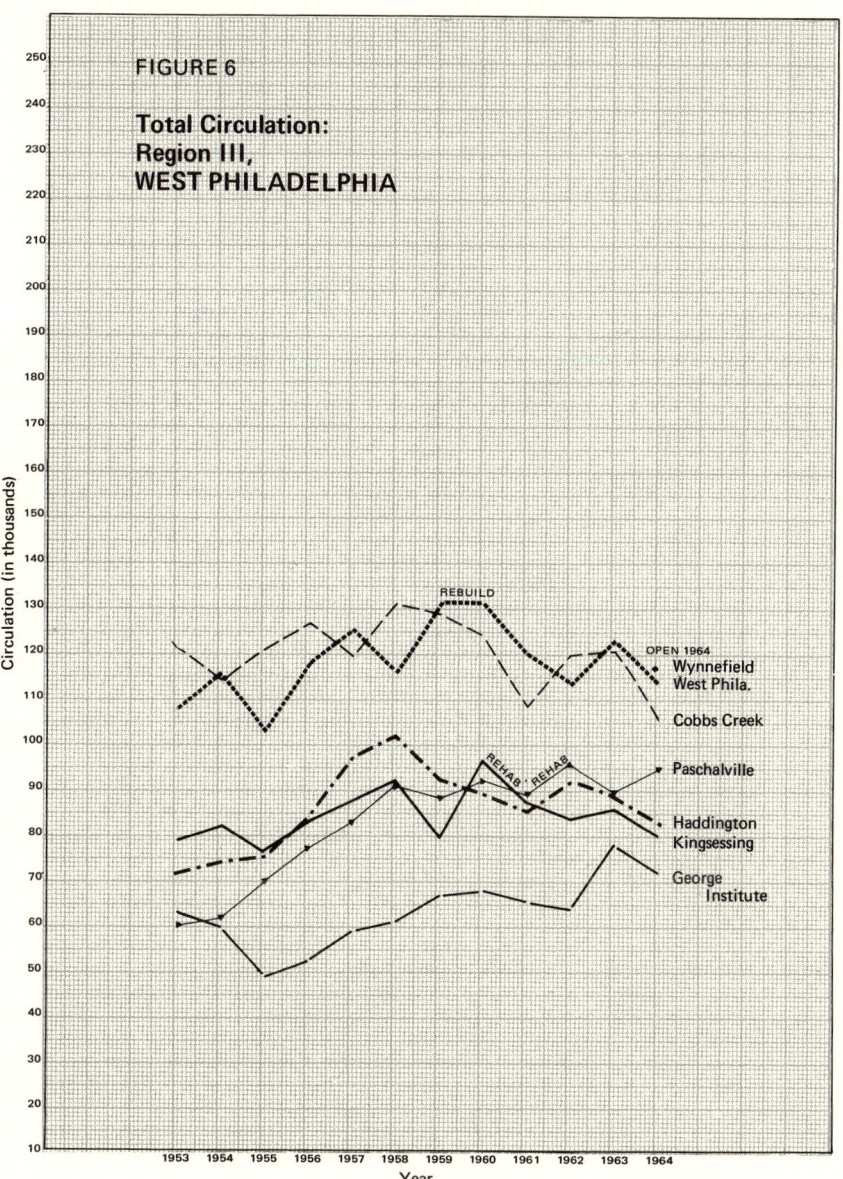

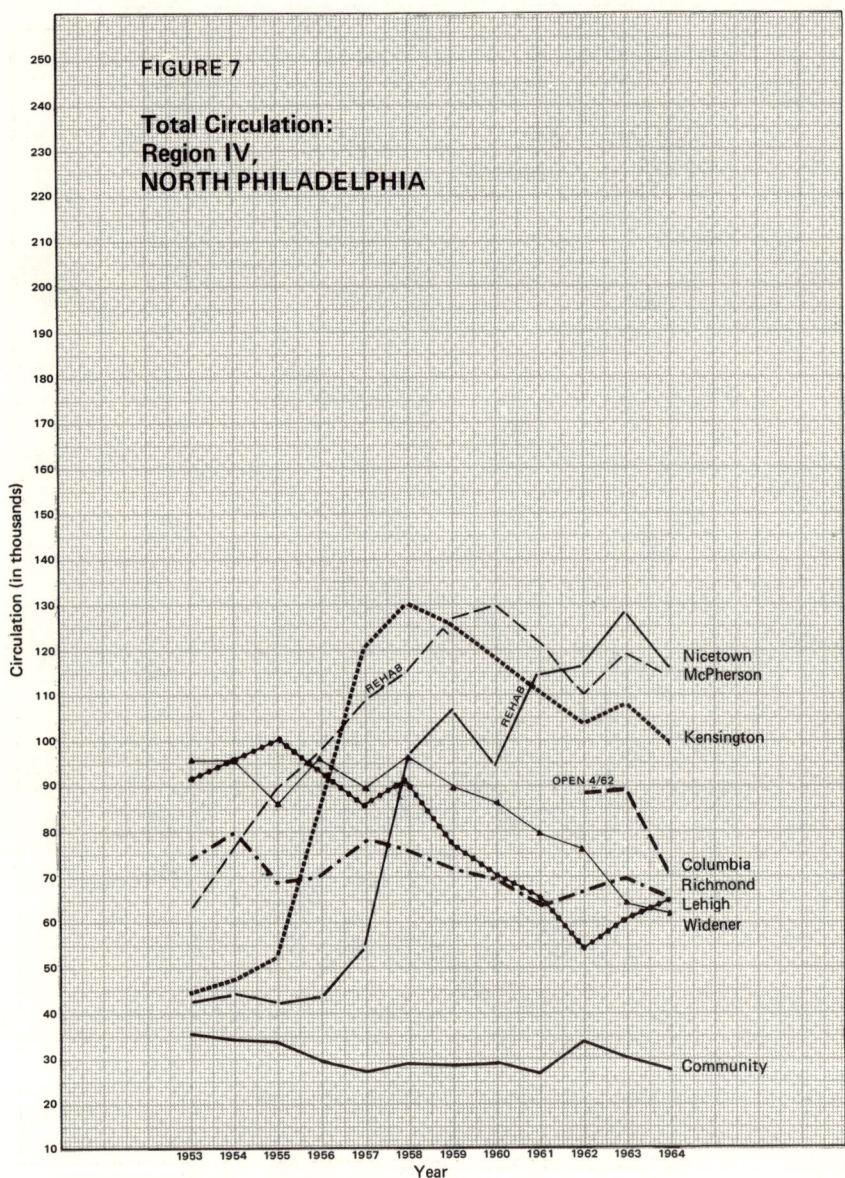

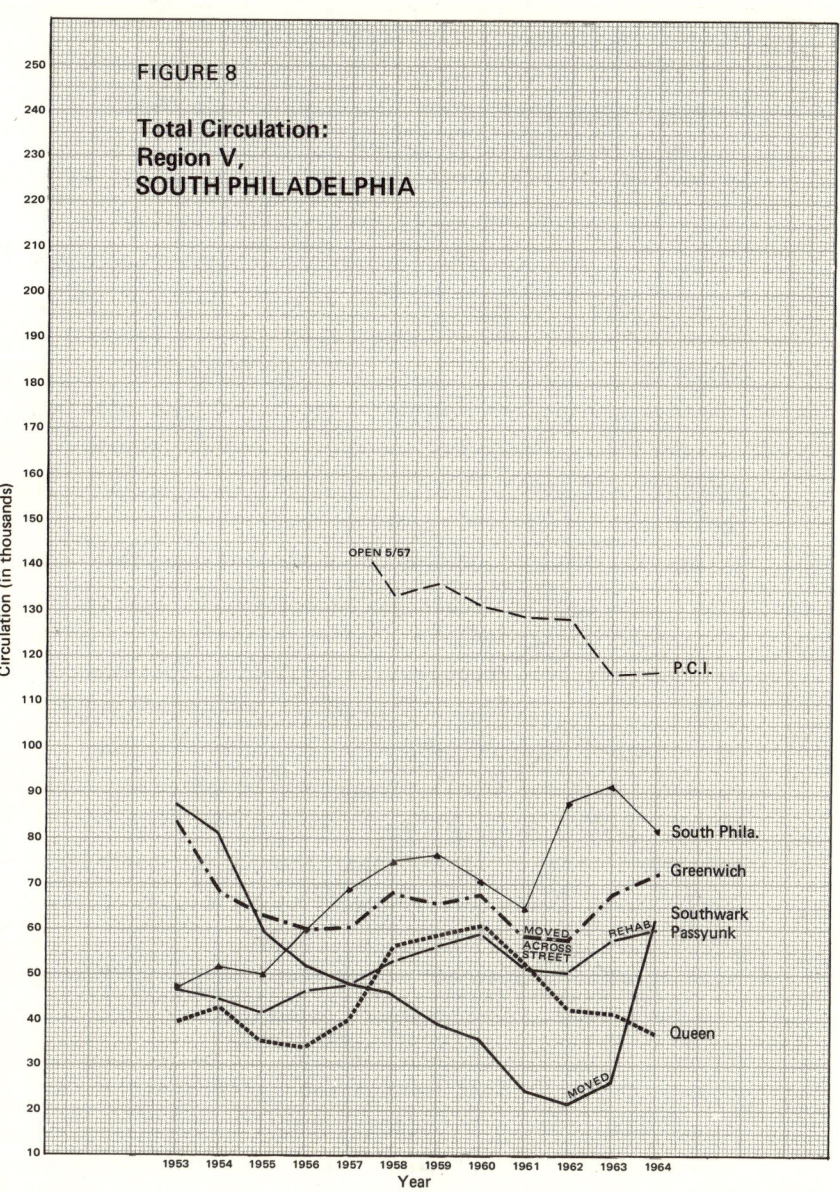

edly drawn off some branch patronage and thus partly explains the drop in branch library circulation in 1964.

Circulation of the individual branches which comprise the system was far from steady, as can be seen in Figures 3–8. (Each figure is for one of the five regions defined by the Free Library. Figures 3–7 are for total circulation. Circulation to juvenile and adult borrowers is given separately in Table 3 for 1961.) The plots for individual branch libraries show rather erratic changes and a wide variation in circulation among branches. The Community Library, at one extreme, had a circulation of only 29,000 in 1960, while the Bushrod Library, at the other extreme, had a circulation of 325,000. The circulation of most libraries was within the range of 80,000–160,000 volumes per year. Even within a given section of the city, no single growth trend is followed by all libraries.

Absolute circulation level is not an adequate measure of how well a library is performing, since it does not take into account the number of potential library users who live close enough to the library to avail themselves of its services. Therefore, the major part of the analysis is based on per capita circulation rather than on absolute circulation. Circulation to adults (persons over fourteen) and to juveniles will be treated separately. For this analysis, service areas used were defined by the branch librarians themselves. These areas are made up of complete census tracts. As a base for computing the adult per capita statistics, we have used the number of persons fifteen years old and over residing within each service area; for juvenile per capita statistics, the number of persons five to fourteen years old has been used.

Since population data were available only from the 1960 census, analysis was restricted to circulation in 1961. Circulation was analyzed for 1961 because during 1960 (and also during

1959) an unusually large number of new and renovated libraries were opening. Data on each of the branch libraries are presented in Table 3; the locations of these libraries are shown in Figure 2.

FACTORS EXPLAINING VARIATIONS IN OUTPUT LEVEL

There appear to be three types of factors that affect the level of library output: the characteristics of the residents in the service area, the quality of the library, and the location of the library.

Characteristics of Residents

Most of the variations in per capita output levels can be explained by the characteristics of the residents in the service area. Three measures were used: median income per household, percentage of people over twenty-five years old with some college education, and percentage of males employed as professionals, managers, or officials. (See columns 17, 18, and 19 of Table 3.) Each of the three is significantly correlated with circulation per capita. (See Table 4.) The percentage of people employed as professionals, managers, or officials, shown in Figures 9 and 10, gives the highest correlations—0.73 for juveniles and 0.86 for adults.

Attempts were made to refine the measure of output to make it reflect the level of professional services as well as the number of books circulated. For adults, the output measure devised was adult circulation plus two times the number of professional services. (See column 10 of Table 3 for number of professional services.) For juveniles, the output measure used was juvenile circulation plus attendance at story hours, book talks, and other library activities in the library, plus two times the attendance at library activities held outside the library. In general, these

TABLE 3

Basic Data on the Branch Library System of the Free Library of Philadelphia, 1960-1961

No.	Branch Name	Most Recent Complete Renovation Year	Type[a]	Floor Space, 1961 (in square feet)	Bookstock, 1961 (in thousands)	Estimated Capital Value, 1961[b] (in thousands of dollars)	Circulation, 1961 (in thousands) Adult	Juvenile	Registration[c] (in hundreds) Adult	Juvenile	Professional Services	Attendance Juvenile Activities in lib.	outside
		1	2	3	4	5	6	7	8	9	10	11	
1	Bushrod	1950	new	7,724	54	370	151	152	125	94	22,511	2,185	5,
2	Bustleton		rented	4,117	32	184	36	37	23	25	2,686	2,508	
3	Chestnut Hill	1958	rehabilitated	6,795	32	299	83	44	48	14	5,832	676	
4	Cobbs Creek	1957	rehabilitated	8,607	33	353	58	50	65	52	6,137	437	
5	Community	1950	rehabilitated	3,059	10	111	8	18	11	17	2,336		
6	Falls	1960	rehabilitated	7,666	24	305	35	34	24	21	3,684	111	1
7	Fox Chase	1951	(in school)	4,917	25	207	50	52	29	23	8,133	10,286	2
8	Frankford	1959	rebuilt	11,852	46	495	137	77	99	56	3,414	2,624	3
9	George Institute	1919	new	3,735	19	123	22	43	29	40	5,454	1,631	4
10	Germantown	1907	new	12,645	31	205	63	35	59	34	4,608	36	
11	Greater Olney	1949	rehabilitated	7,241	39	308	81	55	77	44	3,076	389	4,
12	Greenwich		rented	9,380	27	283	25	32	20	26	2,915	128	1
13	Haddington	1915	new	10,142	29	209	40	45	38	35	5,573	277	1
14	Holmesburg	1959	rehabilitated	8,087	35	433	101	83	72	52	7,052	2,004	1,
15	Kensington	1956	rehabilitated	5,332	32	253	47	64	50	48	12,769	2,069	3.
16	Kingsessing	1961	rehabilitated	8,858	34	377	44	43	38	36	5,233	639	
17	Lehigh	1906	new	12,444	31	137	29	37	49	46	6,267	1,156	
18	Logan	1961	rehabilitated	9,707	36	407	81	53	50	29	4,638	612	2
19	Lovett	1961	rebuilt	8,087	40	413	87	61	43	27	7,375	721	
20	McPherson Square	1958	rehabilitated	9,815	30	381	50	71	44	44	8,439	915	
21	Nicetown-Tioga	1961	rebuilt	9,670	33	391	55	59	58	41	10,613	839	1
22	Oak Lane	1958	rehabilitated	8,071	40	361	103	54	65	25	8,956	1,542	2
23	Paschalville	1915	new	8,984	26	188	42	47	44	38	5,589	1,001	2,
24	Passyunk	1914	new	8,911	19	159	22	30	24	30	1,009		
25	Philadelphia City Institute	1957	new	8,932	34	364	105	23	88	21	5,425	1,383	1
26	Queen Memorial	1957	rehabilitated	2,455	21	137	14	38	28	44	4,001	988	8
27	Richmond	1910	new	9,672	20	155	21	43	23	28	6,372	27	2
28	South Philadelphia	1914	new	8,401	21	160	25	40	41	45	5,378	219	
29	Southwark	1912	new	7,950	30	177	10	14	18	31	4,143	1,388	
30	Tacony	1959	rehabilitated	10,017	29	387	61	72	44	40	3,713	728	3
31	Wadsworth	1959	new	5,943	37	290	88	103	40	22	14,056	931	
32	West Oak Lane	1957	new	7,165	64	406	207	168	129	70	19,269	1,205	1
33	West Philadelphia	1960	rebuilt	10,500	41	445	83	36	94	60	4,471	277	
34	Widener	1946	rebuilt	5,580	30	230	23	56	37	67	4,922	888	
35	Wyoming	1962	rehabilitated	9,623	29	263	39	42	29	23	5,567	204	

[a] "Rebuilt" indicates a substantially greater investment than "rehabilitated." In general, rebuilt libraries were funded through capital programs, and rehabilitated libraries were funded through the operating budget.
[b] See text for method of estimation.
[c] Number of new registrations in 1959 and 1960 and half of registrations in 1958 and 1961. Registration is good for three years.
[d] Accessibility to commercial area = $\sum_{i=1}^{3} \frac{A_i}{d_i^2}$ where A_i is commercial land area in d_i and

$0 < d_1 < 0.05$ mi.; 0.05 mi. $< d_2 < 0.10$ mi.; and 0.10 mi. $< d_3 < 1.5$ mi. Data on commercial area is measured from the Philadelphia City Planning Commission's 1959 land use maps. Commercial area is defined as areas indicated on the land use map as retail sales and services, either alone or with residences above the first floor, offices, and parking.

	Location			Median Income per Household, 1960[f] (in dollars)	Persons over 25 with some College[f] (in percent)	Males Employed as Professionals, Managers Officials[f] (in percent)	Per Capita Circulation		Registered Population (in percent)	
essibility ercial area[d]	Miles to Nearest Library	Miles to Next Nearest Library	Accessibility to School[e]				Adult[g]	Juvenile[h]	Adult[g]	Juvenile[h]
.3	14	15	16	17	18	19	20	21	22	23
.4	1.3	2.4	33	7,160	11.3	26.4	6.7	26.1	53.3	>100
.9	3.4	4.4	54	7,600	19.6	34.4	3.6	11.9	23.3	78.5
.3	2.0	2.7	56	8,549	35.8	46.0	11.2	40.1	65.0	>100
.2	1.2	2.4	6	6,114	12.4	17.0	2.4	8.6	27.0	89.3
.6	1.4	1.1	64	5,743	2.8	7.8	0.9	8.2	12.5	78.1
.4	2.2	2.8	88	6,000	20.5	29.4	4.0	15.5	27.3	95.0
.7	3.7	3.9	190	7,523	12.4	26.4	6.1	32.4	35.3	>100
.3	1.7	2.1	29	6,114	8.5	16.0	4.3	12.4	31.4	91.0
.1	1.25	2.2	86	5,521	14.1	14.4	1.6	13.4	20.5	>100
.2	1.7	1.8	131	6,043	190	21.8	1.3	4.1	12.6	39.8
.3	0.9	1.5	11	6,526	9.1	17.8	2.4	11.1	22.1	87.7
.2	0.8	0.9	86	5,421	3.3	11.9	0.7	3.2	5.8	26.0
.9	1.25	2.3	104	5,379	9.2	11.6	1.0	4.9	9.0	38.0
.6	1.7	3.1	88	7,069	10.1	21.0	4.8	15.9	34.4	98.0
.1	0.9	1.0	80	5,072	3.4	6.9	2.5	11.9	23.6	89.5
.5	1.2	1.4	65	5,945	9.2	15.7	1.5	6.6	12.5	56.5
.7	0.9	1.4	18	4,904	2.7	6.2	1.3	5.7	21.8	71.3
.7	0.9	1.8	158	6,366	14.1	27.4	5.0	25.0	30.9	>100
.7	1.4	1.7	4	7,810	31.5	36.4	3.8	12.4	18.8	55.0
.6	0.8	1.0	63	5,692	3.7	10.6	1.7	10.6	15.4	65.9
.3	1.8	2.1	120	5,170	8.9	11.4	1.6	8.9	16.5	61.0
.7	1.7	1.8	58	7,109	20.7	38.6	6.4	17.4	35.9	79.4
.5	2.2	2.4	61	6,316	5.2	11.8	2.4	11.1	24.5	89.5
.3	0.7	1.1	44	5,711	5.5	13.2	0.7	3.8	7.3	39.0
.3	0.8	1.1	11	8,000	36.4	45.5	6.7	23.0	56.0	>100
.7	1.1	1.1	53	4,400	2.7	5.6	0.7	6.9	13.2	80.5
.1	0.8	1.1	26	5,945	4.1	8.6	1.6	15.9	18.5	>100
.7	0.7	0.3	25	5,230	4.5	11.1	1.2	10.7	19.7	>100
.2	0.8	1.4	188	4,310	4.2	10.0	0.5	3.0	9.0	65.5
.0	1.7	2.3	43	6,624	7.8	17.0	2.1	10.9	15.4	62.0
.6	1.4	1.7	21	7,625	24.6	41.2	7.5	29.0	34.5	62.7
.8	1.4	1.8	37	7,198	21.5	34.6	7.1	28.1	44.0	>100
.5	1.4	2.4	11	4,936	27.0	29.0	3.5	17.6	40.1	>100
.5	1.8	2.1	69	5,409	4.1	8.1	0.9	7.9	14.7	95.9
.3	1.5	2.0	133	6,100	5.3	15.0	2.9	18.9	22.1	>100

[e]Index resulting from the following operations: $\frac{1}{10 \times 8^{-2}}$ ([sum of number of pupils divided by distance squared for elementary schools] plus [sum of number of pupils divided by distance for junior high schools]). The schools are both public and parochial with 1/2 mile radius from library for elementary schools and 3/4 mile for junior high schools. Distances are taken with 1/8 mile unit.

[f]Data from U.S. Census of Population: 1960 for census tracts. Where necessary, a weighted average of medians of several tracts was taken.

[g]Columns 6 and 8, respectively, divided by the number of residents fifteen years old and over in nominal service area.

[h]Columns 7 and 9, respectively, divided by the number of residents from five to fourteen years old in nominal service area.

TABLE 4

Library Output and Characteristics of Residents in Nominal Service Area: Correlation Coefficients

Dependent Variable (Output)	Independent Variable (Characteristics of Residents)		
	Occupational Level[a]	Educational Level[b]	Median Income
Adult per capita circulation	0.86	0.73	0.81
Adult per capita circulation + 2x professional services	0.82	0.69	0.81
Juvenile per capita circulation	0.73	0.60	0.72
Juvenile per capita circulation + attendance at library activities + 2x attendance at library activities outside library	0.69	low[c]	low[c]

[a]Percent of adult males employed as professionals, managers, or officials.
[b]Percent of people over twenty-five years old with some college education.
[c]Necessary minimum size of correlation coefficient for significance at 0.05 level is 0.32; for significance at 0.01 level, it is 0.42.

redefinitions of library output resulted in lower correlations with the characteristics of the residents than did output defined simply as circulation. Higher weightings on the auxiliary outputs would probably result in even lower correlations. Circulation alone, therefore, appears to be the "better" measure of library output, in that it can be explained more consistently by the characteristics of residents in the service area of the library.

The socioeconomic characteristics of the residents in the nominal service area thus seem to account for most library output, no matter which of the three specific variables is used to describe these characteristics. Although the correlation coefficients for juveniles are lower than those for adults, they all have high statistical significance.

The explanation provided by the socioeconomic characteristics of the residents is so strong that one might argue that library

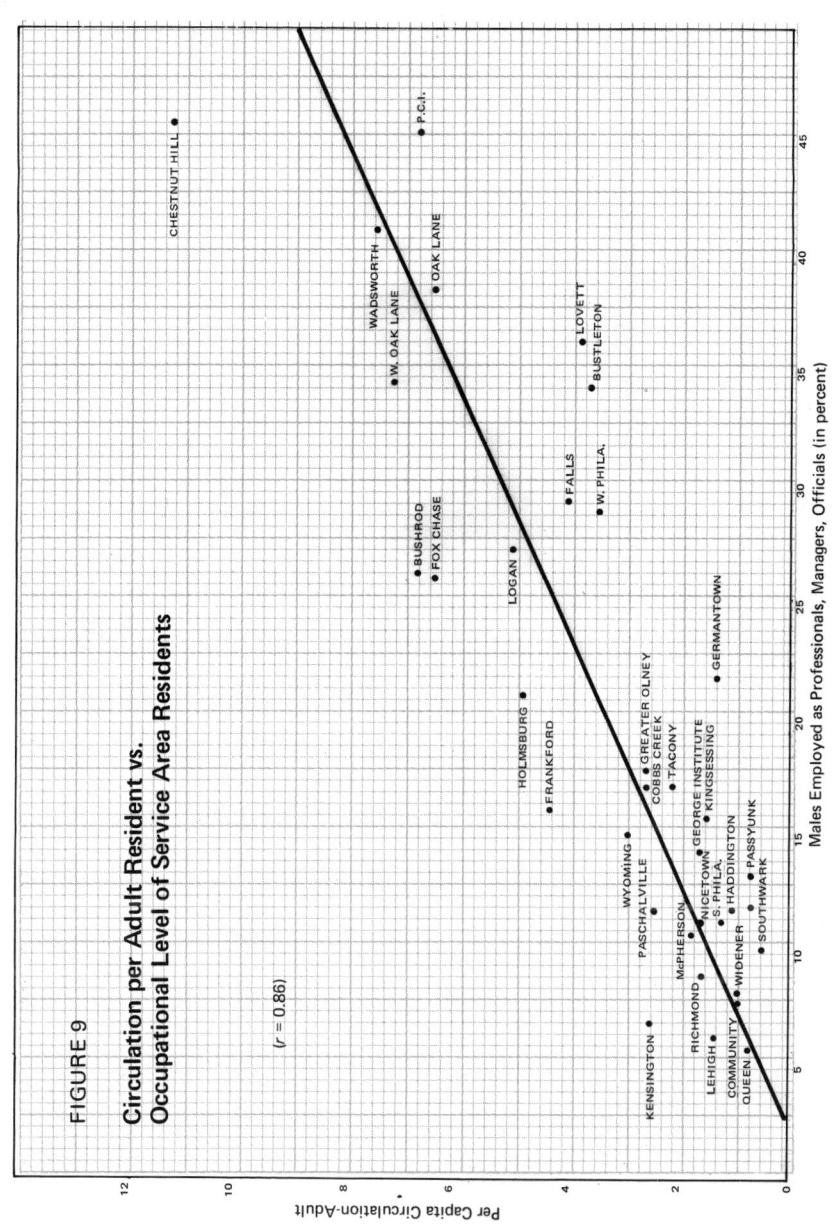

FIGURE 9
Circulation per Adult Resident vs. Occupational Level of Service Area Residents

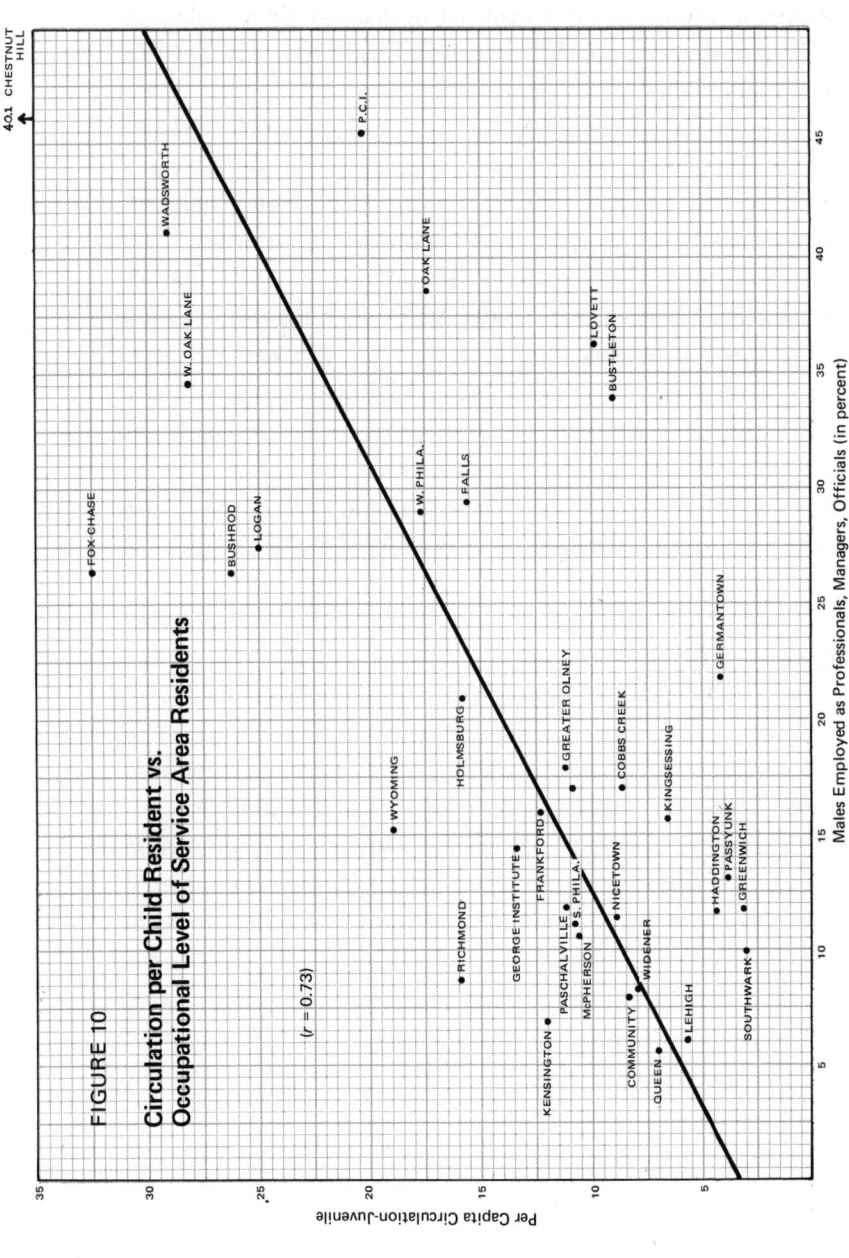

Output of Individual Branches

service is determined almost entirely by demand. Branch libraries responding solely to neighborhood demand appear, then, to be consistent with a goal of maximizing circulation.

If other community goals, such as those presented in Figure 1, are relevant, however, simple response to demand may not be an appropriate policy. If, as the statistical evidence suggests, output is heavily determined by population characteristics over which the library planner has no control, then it may be difficult for the planner to increase library use through the manipulation of factors that he does control, such as size, location, and quality. Nevertheless, it is essential to determine whether library utilization by less educated, poorer, or less skilled residents can be increased through system policies. One approach to this determination is to investigate the residual variance in library use which is not explained by the socioeconomic characteristics of residents.

Quality of Library

One would expect the quality of the bookstock, the quality of the staff, and the attractiveness of the library building itself to have a major effect upon circulation per capita. Quality is an elusive concept, however, and its measurement is difficult.

A number of measures of quality were used in attempts to explain the deviation of per capita circulation from the expected value based on occupational level of the residents of the nominal service area. The first and most successful measure was the number of books in each library. Correlation of bookstock of each library with the deviation from the circulation expected for the occupational level of its service area resulted in a coefficient of correlation of 0.238. (See Figure 11.)[1]

This result is not statistically significant. In addition, the number of books in each library is not a logically satisfying

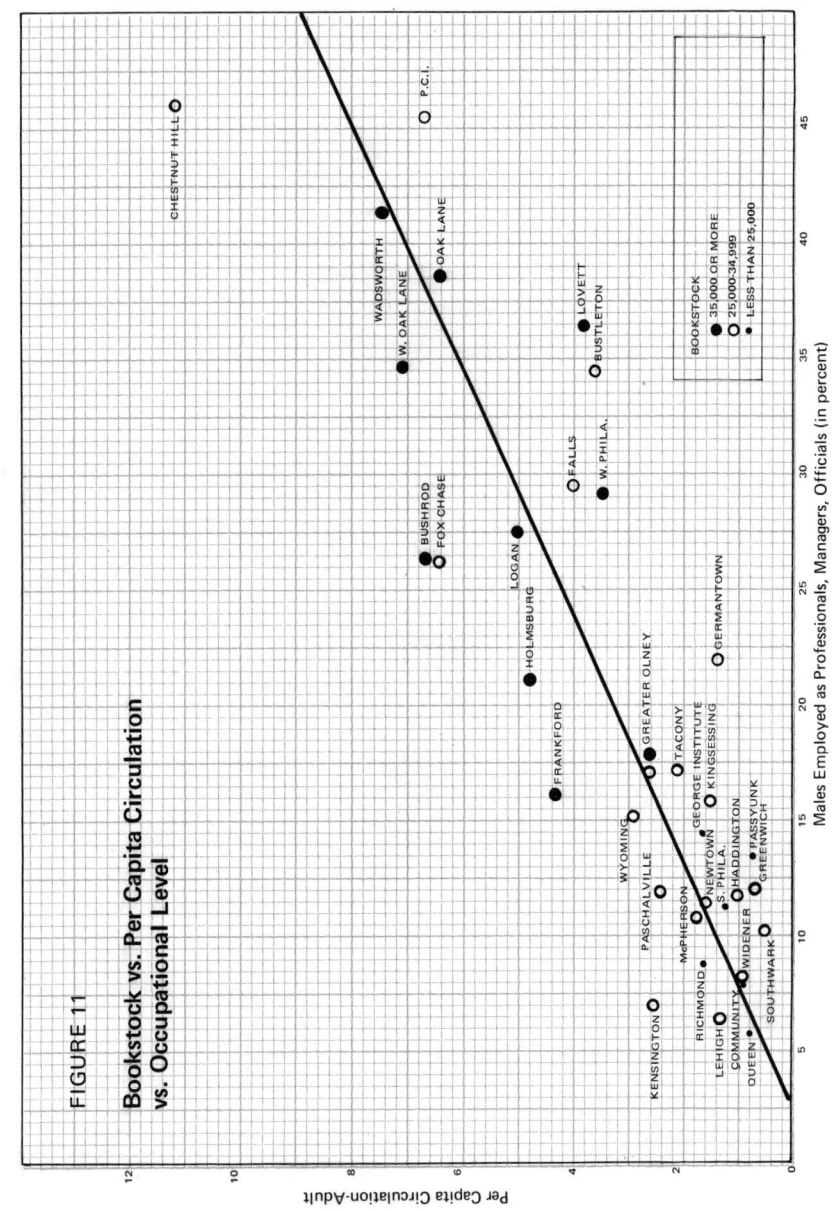

Output of Individual Branches

measure since one would expect that the quality of bookstock could vary from library to library and could be independent of the number of books in each library. The only known measure of quality of bookstock is an evaluation made by the Free Library's coordinator for work with adults. This evaluation, which gave a rating between zero and ten, was found to vary systematically with bookstock size, but also to have a considerable range of values for any given bookstock size. The deviations of these ratings from the regression line based on bookstock, however, bear no systematic relation to the deviations of circulation from the regression line based on occupational level. Therefore, adjustment of bookstock by the quality rating would not appear to improve the correlation obtained by bookstock alone.

A second attempt to measure quality involved a general quality rating used by the library coordinator. This rating is made up of the bookstock rating discussed previously in addition to ratings on nine other items, such as staff, use of books in the library, registration trend, circulation trend, and population trend. Each item is marked from zero to ten; the higher the mark, the more urgent the need of money or the lower the quality of the library. The items are weighted (the first three receiving the most weight) and then added to produce the rating for budget use.

For this analysis, total number of books (bookstock) was divided by the budget rating. The resulting index can be thought of as a measure of the attractiveness of the library, weighted by size. The index is low for a library in urgent need of a budget increase and higher for a library in less need of additional funds. The resulting measure is not reliable as a continuous measure, but the extremes should have some significance.

Of the libraries rating very high, Frankford and West Oak

Lane had higher circulations than expected for the socioeconomic characteristics of their service areas; however, West Philadelphia, Lovett, and West Oak Lane had lower circulations than expected. Of the libraries rating very low, Passyunk, South Philadelphia, Southwark, George Institute, and Bustleton had lower circulations than expected, while Kensington and Wadsworth had higher circulations than expected. Therefore, the measure of attractiveness does not appear to provide an adequate explanation of variation in library circulation for a given occupational level of community residents. Perhaps this failure was due, in part, to the fact that the current (1966) budget rating was used in the attempt to explain variation in 1961 circulation. Data from which one might construct a comparable measure of library quality for 1961 are no longer available.

The presence of a children's librarian was used as an indicator of quality in order to explain variations in juvenile circulation. In nine libraries, no children's librarian was assigned; in the Germantown branch, a children's librarian was assigned only for four months; in all other branches, a children's librarian was assigned for twelve months. Libraries without a children's librarian generally tend to have smaller juvenile circulation than would be expected on the basis of occupational level, as seen in Figure 12. Libraries with a children's librarian, however, appear to be equally likely to have higher or lower per capita circulation than that expected. Therefore, the presence or absence of a children's librarian does not provide an adequate statistical explanation of variations in per capita circulation.

Finally, another general measure related to quality was investigated: the capital value of the library. It seems reasonable to suppose that there would be a correlation between total investment in a library facility and the service provided by the library. Comprehensive data on investment, however, are diffi-

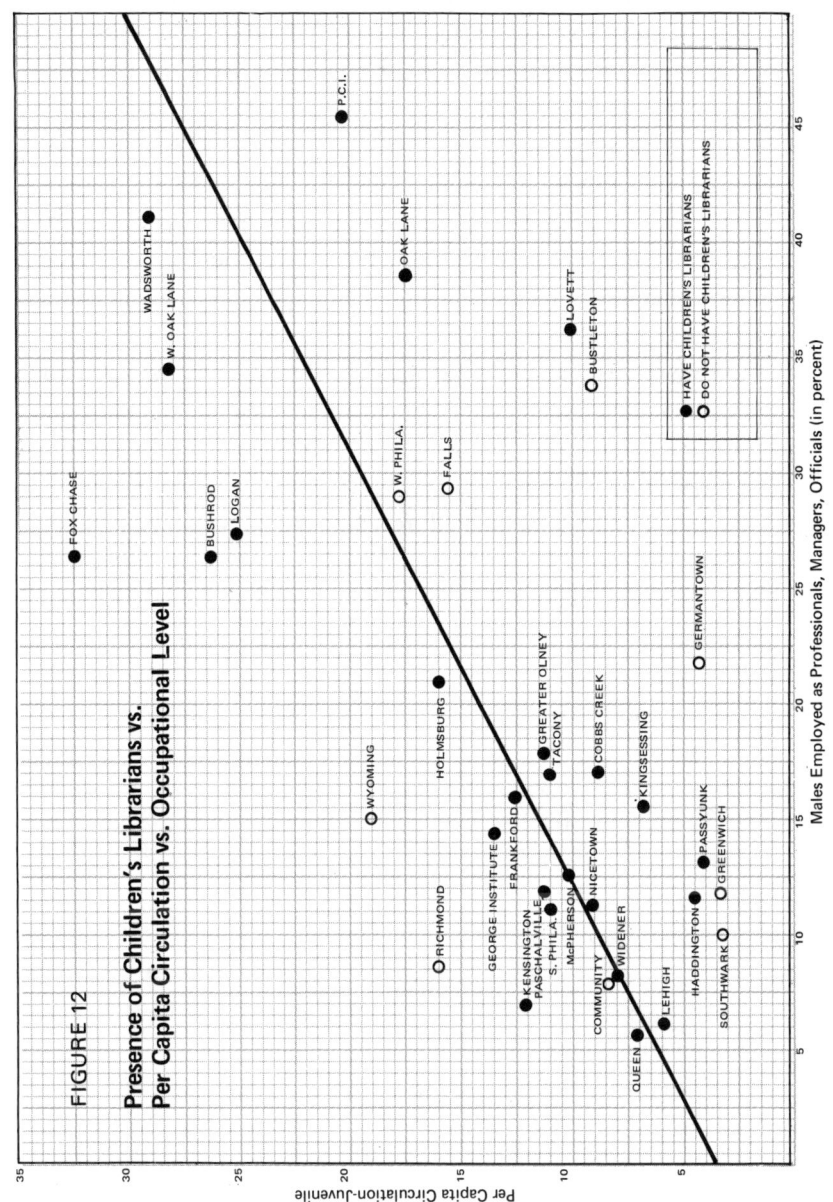

cult to obtain and to interpret. Initial investments for the various libraries have been made during a period of fifty years, and data on these investments are not readily available. In addition, most libraries have been thoroughly renovated or rebuilt since their first construction.

In order to get comparable investment figures for the various branches, an estimate of present value was made on the assumption that at the time of its most recent renovation or rebuilding each library was in an essentially "new" condition. (See columns 1 and 2, Table 3.) Present value of investment is defined as the investment in building space (assumed to be $30.53 per square foot) depreciated by the number of years since the building was "new," plus investment in bookstock.[2] Straight-line depreciation to the value of zero over seventy-five years was assumed. Libraries in rented quarters were considered to be twenty-five years old to account for the fact that rented quarters are generally regarded as unsatisfactory. (For floor space and bookstock, see columns 3 and 4, Table 3.)

There is little evidence of strong correlation between the present estimated value of investment in the library and the deviation from the regression line of circulation and occupational level. (See Figures 9 and 10.) The correlation coefficient (0.170) is positive, as would be expected, but is too low for statistical significance.

Location of Library

The location of a library, particularly in relation to other facilities, generally is believed to have an important influence upon library use.

The closeness of a library to a shopping area is generally considered to be the most important factor in adult circulation. The possibility of combining a visit to the library with a

Output of Individual Branches

shopping trip can encourage regular users to visit the library more often, and convenient location of a library in a commercial area may attract some shoppers who would not ordinarily have thought of using it. The availability of nearby parking in a commercial area may also lead to increased use of a library located in such an area. On the other hand, congestion and lack of parking spaces in some commercial areas may discourage use of a library.

Data are available on areas of land in commercial use, but not on the intensity of commercial activity or the level of congestion in such areas. The areas of commercial land use, shown on maps of the Philadelphia City Planning Commission, were measured and classified by distance "rings" around each library.[3] (The rings were usually diamond-shaped since all distances were measured along streets, which are typically in a rectangular grid pattern.) An accessibility measure was formed by dividing the area in commercial use in each ring by the square of the average distance to the ring and then summing. The results and details of computation are given in column 13, Table 3.

In Figure 13, each library is classified by the quartile in which its commercial index falls. Those in the highest quartile have the highest commercial indexes and would be expected to lie above the regression line. Those in the lowest quartile would be expected to lie below the line. To a lesser extent, those in the second quartile would be expected to lie above the line and those in the third quartile below the line. Inspection of Figure 13 indicates that no such relationship holds. The correlation between the commercial accessibility index and the deviation from the expected per capita circulation was not computed because it is evident that it is low.

Since a major component of adult circulation is circulation to young adults, one might expect that the closeness of the li-

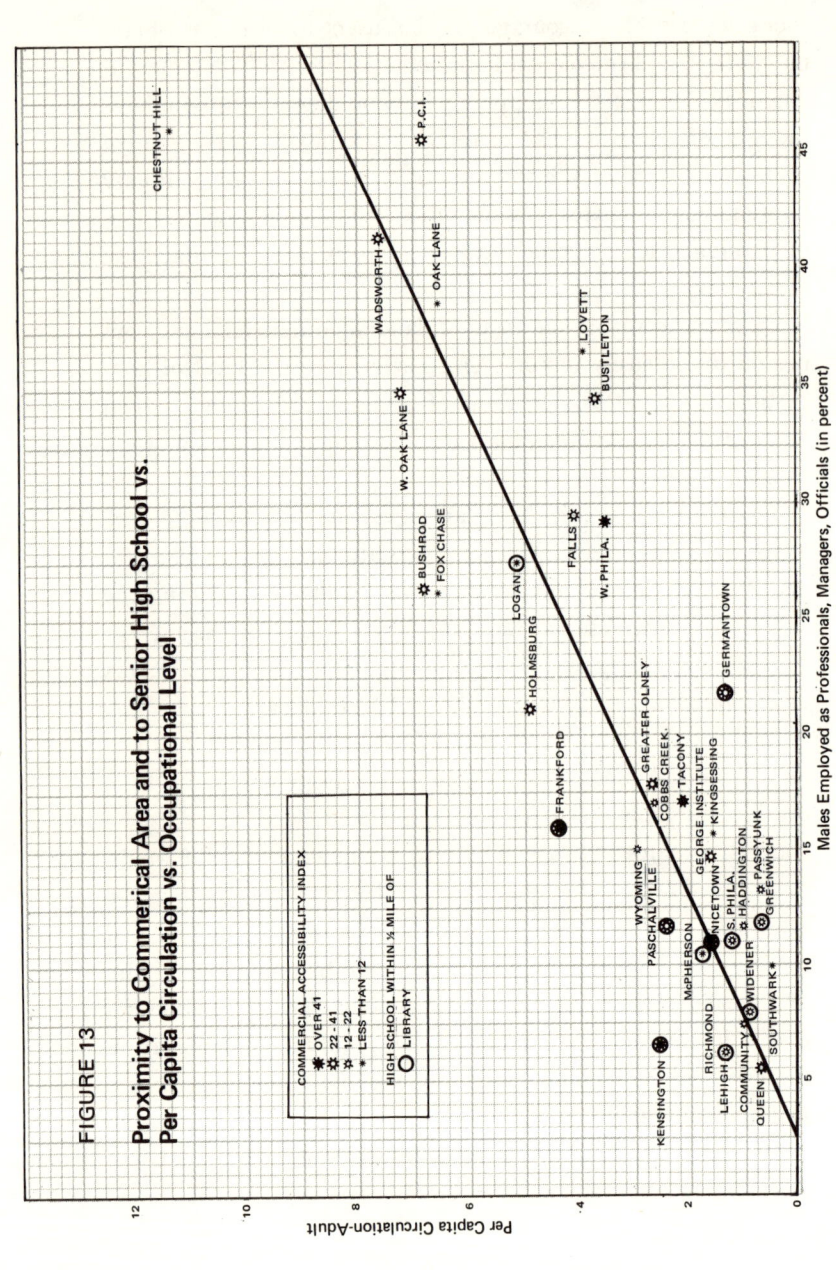

FIGURE 13
Proximity to Commercial Area and to Senior High School vs. Per Capita Circulation vs. Occupational Level

Output of Individual Branches 53

brary to high schools would have an effect upon circulation. The ten libraries within a half mile of senior high schools are also marked on Figure 13. These, too, have no apparent pattern. In fact, the statistical analysis suggests that the closeness of a senior high school would reduce per capita circulation rather than increase it. Such a conclusion, however, lacks statistical significance. (A correlation coefficient of -0.117 was obtained.)

In summary, it appears that neither proximity to commercial areas nor proximity to high schools provided a significant explanation of why a particular library has a larger or smaller per capita adult circulation than would be expected on the basis of the occupational level of the residents in its service area. These data do not provide a justification for the incurring extra land cost of being near schools or commercial areas.

Accessibility to elementary and junior high schools is considered to be a major factor in juvenile circulation, whereas accessibility to commercial areas is considered to be less important than it is for adult circulation. A measure of the accessibility of libraries to schools was constructed by dividing the number of pupils enrolled in each school by the distance to the library, and summing over schools. In Figure 14, three categories are designated: libraries that have schools that are relatively large or relatively near; libraries that have schools that are relatively small or relatively far; and an intermediate class. Following our hypothesis, one would expect that, for any given occupational level of the population, libraries in a given school proximity class would have a higher circulation than those in lower school proximity classes. This effect is not altogether clear from the graph, and the analysis failed to show a statistically significant relationship. (See Table 5.)

Specifically, four variations of the basic measure of accessibil-

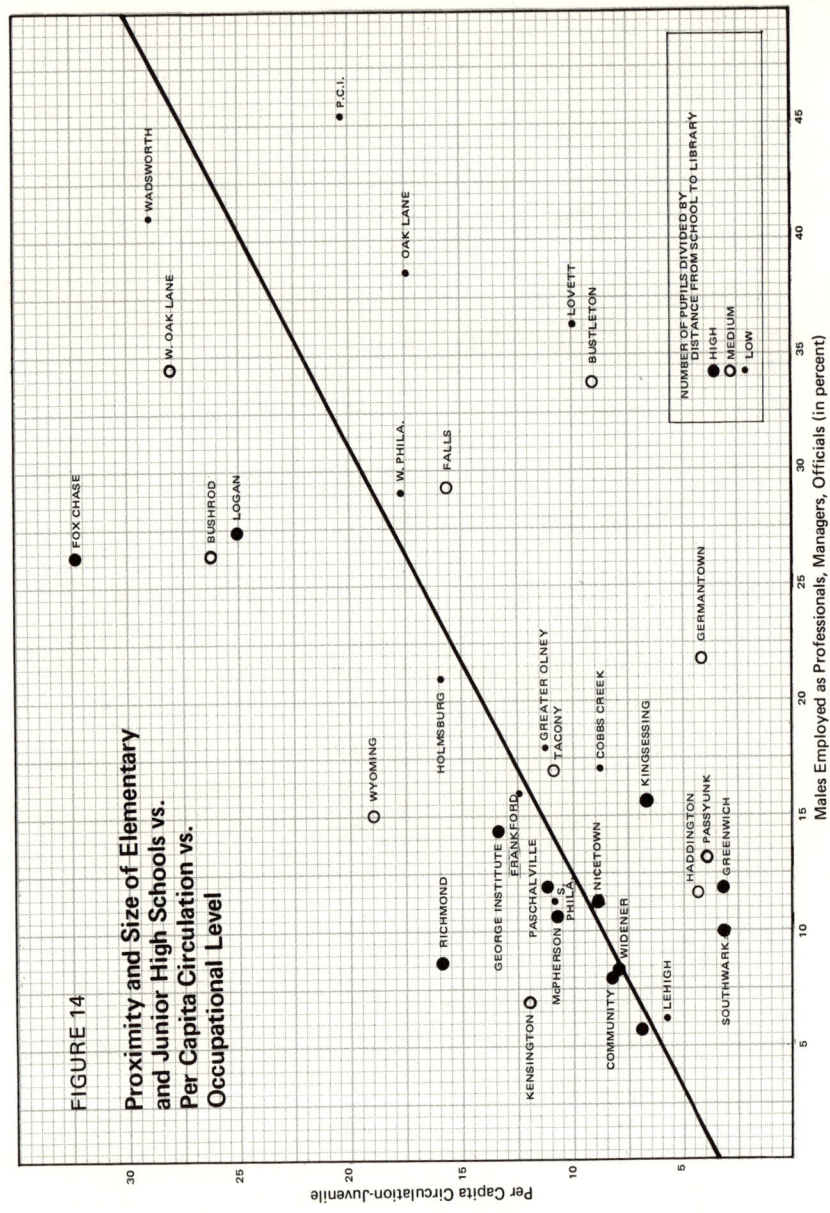

Output of Individual Branches

TABLE 5

Correlations between Accessibility to Schools and Deviation from Expected Juvenile Circulation, for Various Measures of Proximity

	Accessibility Measure	Coefficient of Correlation between Accessibility and Deviations, r[a]
1	$\sum \frac{\text{number of pupils}}{\text{distance}}$ (Elementary + secondary school)	0.130
2	$\sum \frac{\text{number of pupils}}{(\text{distance})^2}$ (Elementary school)	0.135
3[b]	$\sum \frac{\text{number of pupils}}{(\text{distance})^2}$ (Elementary school) + $\sum \frac{\text{number of pupils}}{\text{distance}}$ (Secondary school)	0.143
4	$\sum \frac{\text{number of pupils}}{(\text{distance})^3}$ (Elementary school)	0.117

[a] Deviations are those from the expected value of juvenile per capita circulation determined by the regression with occupational level.
[b] Data are given in Table 3, column 16.

ity to schools were tried. None provided a statistically significant explanation for the variation in juvenile per capita circulation from the average levels based on the social and economic character of the residents in the service area. (See Table 5.)

Relationship between Adult and Juvenile Circulation

It has been suggested that teen-age library users are so noisy that they discourage the patronage of adults. Figure 15 indicates that, on the contrary, juvenile patronage is positively associated with adult patronage. The correlation between per capita adult circulation and per capita juvenile circulation is extremely high ($r = 0.92$). This is by far the highest correlation achieved in

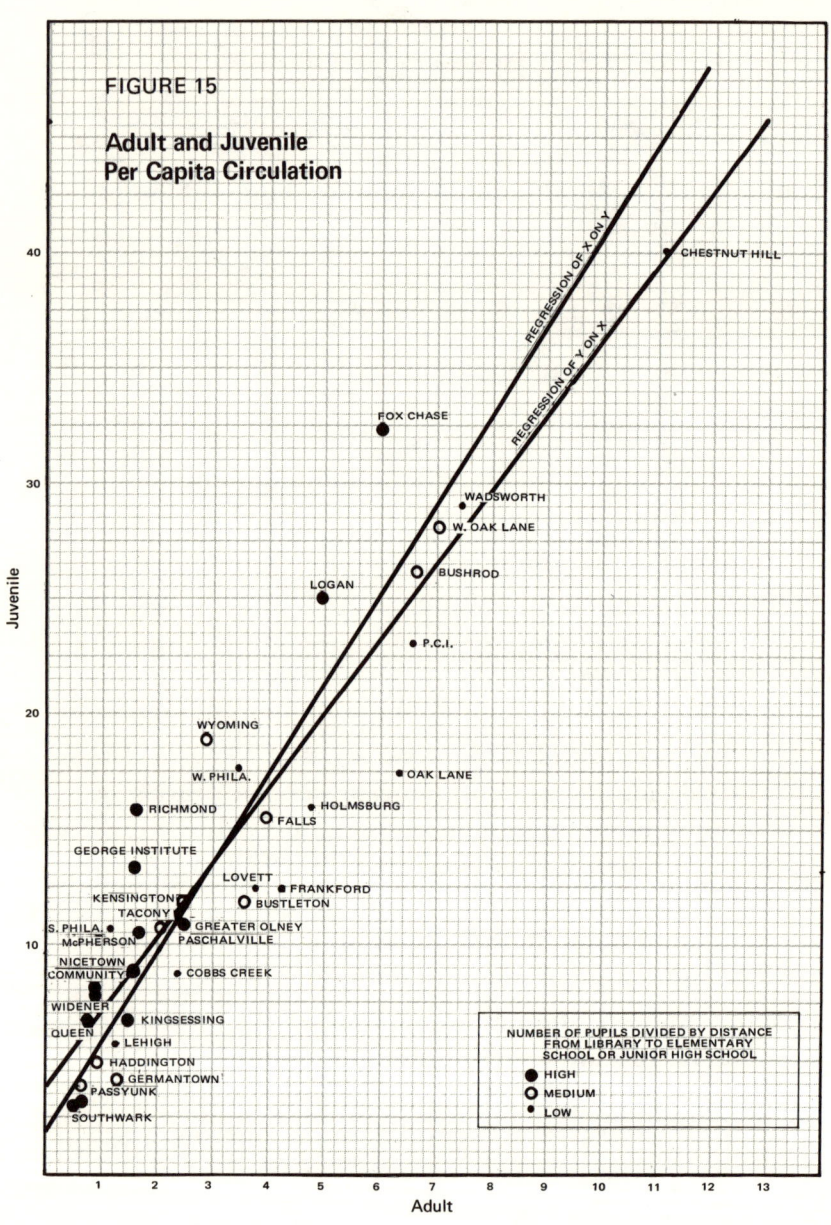

Output of Individual Branches 57

the entire analysis. It suggests the conclusion that, in a community, children and adults have similar cultural patterns and that these similar patterns are more important to adult patronage than the effects of children's noise and disruption. By itself, however, this finding is of limited practical value because it does not indicate whether library use could be increased by a change in the habits of the children or by a change in the habits of the adults.

Figure 15 provides another opportunity for explaining the deviation of individual libraries from the expected levels of circulation. To attempt to explain variations in adult per capita circulation for a given juvenile per capita circulation, we used the proximity of commercial areas and of senior high schools. Once again neither correlation was significant.

To explain variations in juvenile per capita circulation for a given adult per capita circulation, the accessibility of elementary and junior high schools was used. These are marked on the graph. The coefficient of correlation (0.24) was virtually as high as the minimum necessary for significance at a 10 percent level (0.28). Therefore, one probably should not reject the hypothesis that an increase in juvenile circulation would result from proximity of libraries to schools.

SUMMARY

In summary, the analysis of data normally collected by the Free Library of Philadelphia indicates that social and economic characteristics of the residents of a library's service area determine, to a large extent, the use that will be made of the library. Available measures of the quality of a library do not provide a statistically adequate explanation of deviations from the use level expected on the basis of social and economic characteristics of residents. Neither bookstock, nor quality rating, nor quality rating corrected by bookstock, nor budget-needs rating, nor presence of a children's librarian, nor capital value of the library explain the deviations from the expected per capita use. Measures of the specific location of the library—in relation to commercial areas and senior high schools for adult circulation, and in relation to elementary and junior high schools for juveniles —also failed to provide a statistically significant explanation of the deviations.

NOTES

1. Note that the basic data and regression lines plotted in Figures 11 through 14 are the same as those plotted in Figures 9 and 10. The purpose of Figures 11 through 14 is to explain the deviations from the regression line. Ratings of each library on variables intended to explain the deviations are indicated by various symbols, which are identified in the key to each figure.

2. Unit costs were based on recent data provided by the Free Library and other sources.

3. Size and areal extent of major commercial areas are given also in a 1959 *Philadelphia Inquirer* report, "Delaware Valley Shopping Centers." These data, however, do not cover commercial areas even as large as the Chestnut Hill commercial area. Only fifteen of the thirty-five branch libraries were found to fall within commercial areas as defined by the *Inquirer* study.

5

THE INDIVIDUAL BRANCH: A DETAILED SURVEY

The results of the analysis of available data are disappointing in that they do not provide us with a substantially improved basis for planning a library system. We can certainly say that if the goal is simply higher circulation, libraries should be placed in neighborhoods inhabited by a high percentage of professionals, managers, or officials, or, alternatively, by people with a high median income or a high level of educational attainment. However, the analysis has not invalidated the argument that it is advantageous to locate libraries close to schools or in commercial areas.

It is possible that there actually is little correlation between the proximity of a library to schools or commercial concentrations and the service rendered by the library. However, the failure of the analysis to uncover such correlations may be attributable to the coarseness of the data analyzed.

In a number of respects, the available data might be judged inadequate for providing answers to the questions posed:

1. Per capita measurements were based upon service areas as defined by branch librarians from their general knowledge.

Even if these service areas proved to be very good approximations of the actual service areas of the libraries, per capita measurements based on them would still be unsatisfactory. This is because these measurements are averages over the area and take no account of the obvious fact that even within the nominal service area library circulation falls off with distance from user's residence to the library.

2. The data on both age and occupation are averages for all residents in entire census tracts and do not describe the specific users of the library.

3. Even if the data indicated that a relationship exists between location in a commercial area and the level of library output, it would be impossible to identify the nature of the relationship. That is, it would be impossible to know whether users make combined library-shopping trips or whether they are simply taking advantage of convenient public transportation or parking space in the commercial area.

4. Circulation was used as a general measure of output based on the observation that there is some correlation between circulation and the number of professional services. However, it is not known whether the people who take out books tend also to use other library services provided by the professional staff or whether these services are used primarily by other library patrons.

In short, our measure of output leaves much to be desired. In order to overcome these deficiencies and to achieve useful results for planning purposes, a direct survey was made of library users. Seven Philadelphia branch libraries were chosen from neighborhoods of varying socioeconomic levels and from locations with high and low accessibilities to commercial areas. In addition, one branch (Wynnefield) was chosen from those in medium-density neighborhoods near the city boundary. (See Table 6 and Figure 16.)

TABLE 6

Branch Libraries, by Location and Type of Neighborhood

Proximity to Commercial Areas	Characteristics of Neighborhood		
	Lower Class	Lower Middle Class	Upper Middle Class
High	Columbia[a] George Institute Kensington Nicetown Queen Memorial	Falls Frankford[a] Greater Olney Roxborough Tacony West Philadelphia	Bushrod Holmesburg Wadsworth[a] West Oak Lane Wynnefield[a]
Low	Community Greenwich Richmond[a] Lehigh McPherson Square Passyunk South Philadelphia Southwark Widener	Cobbs Creek Haddington[a] Kingsessing Lawncrest Paschalville Wyoming	Chestnut Hill Fox Chase Logan Lovett[a] Oak Lane

[a]Libraries surveyed.

TABLE 7

Characteristics of Residents of Nominal Service Areas, 1960

	Median Income per Household (in dollars)	Persons over 25 with Some College (in percent)	Males Employed as Professionals, Managers, Officials (in percent)
Columbia	3,830	4.9	4.9
Richmond	5,945	4.1	8.6
Haddington	5,379	9.2	11.6
Frankford	6,114	8.5	16.0
Lovett	7,810	31.5	36.4
Wadsworth	7,625	24.6	41.2
Wynnefield	7,598	22.7	41.4

Note: Service areas defined by the Free Library of Philadelphia as in Chapter 4.

Source: Data from U.S. Census of Population: 1960.

Income, education, and occupational characteristics of the residents of service areas are given in Table 7 for the libraries surveyed. The service areas are those defined by officials of the library system and used previously in the analysis in chapter 4. Each measure gives a slightly different ranking of the library service areas. For Table 7 and subsequent tables, the ranking derived from the occupational group is used. The data on characteristics of residents in service areas is for 1960, since that is the most recent year for which census data are available.

The locations of the libraries surveyed are shown in Figure 16. Also shown are the locations of all libraries in the system as of 1961, the data to which the analysis of chapter 4 refers. Basic data on the physical plant and the output of each library in the survey are given in Table 8. These data are for 1966.

Wynnefield and Frankford stand out as the largest and most active libraries. Wynnefield has the largest floor area and provides the largest number of professional services. Frankford has the largest bookstock, the largest adult and juvenile circulation, and by far the largest attendance at juvenile programs. At the low end of the scale are Haddington and Lovett with the least floor space, Richmond with the smallest bookstock and the smallest number of professional services, Columbia with the smallest circulation, and Wynnefield with the smallest attendance at juvenile programs.

The range in physical plant is considerably narrower than the range in output. The largest floor area is one-and-one-half times the smallest. The range of bookstock is similar. For each measure of output—circulation, professional services, and attendance at juvenile programs—the library with the highest level is about four times the smallest.

In general, it can be seen that circulation and number of professional services increase with the social level of the service

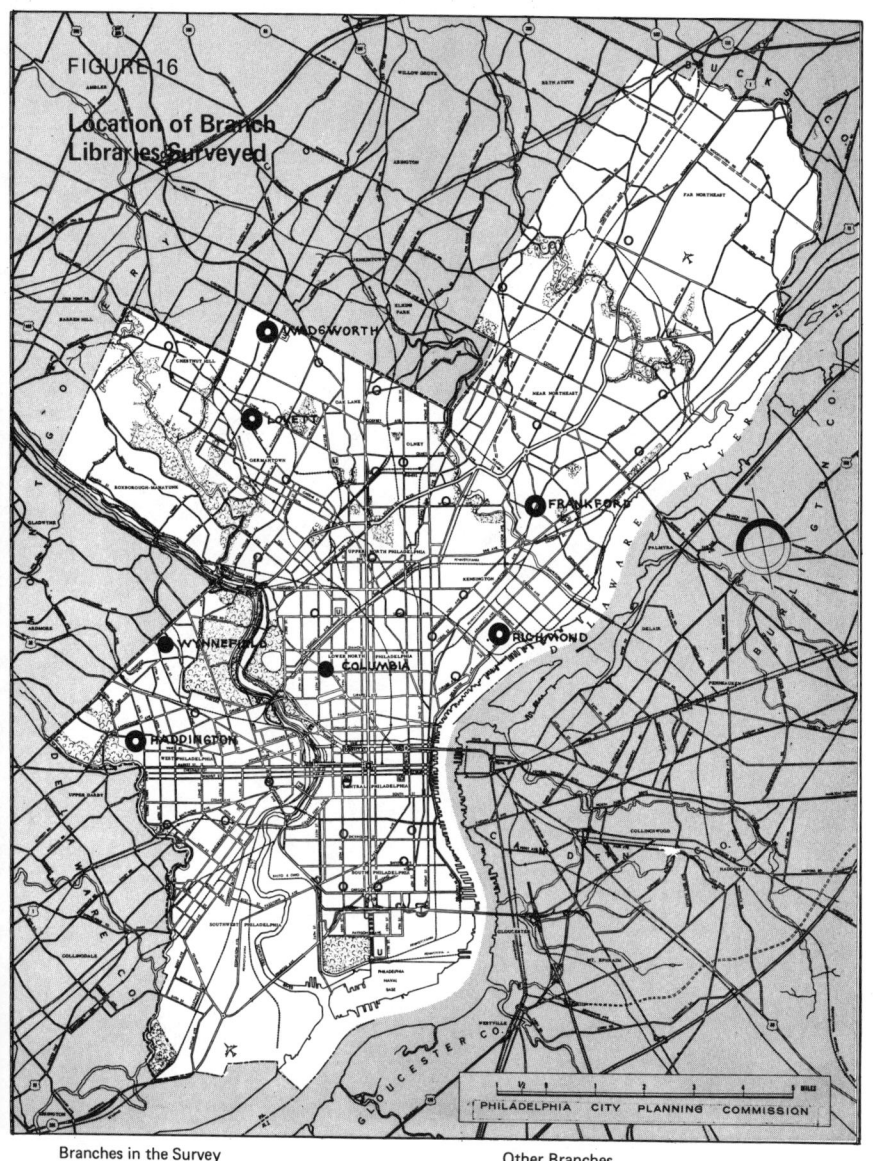

Branches in the Survey
◉ Branches in Operation in 1961
● Branches Built Since 1961

Other Branches
○ Branches in Operation in 1961

TABLE 8

Data on Physical Plant and Output of Branch Libraries, 1966

	Columbia	Richmond	Haddington	Frankford	Lovett	Wadsworth	Wynnefield
Physical plant [a]							
Floor space (in square feet)	8,550	9,672	8,087	11,852	8,087	5,943	13,600
Bookstock	28,316	20,063	23,900	51,402	39,463	38,447	47,693
Capital value [b] (in thousands of dollars)	362	142	196	472	366	290	530
Output [a]							
Adult circulation	19,066	22,245	28,303	127,610	90,269	72,313	126,129
Juvenile circulation	28,195	37,740	36,015	79,000	64,913	68,142	71,191
Total circulation	47,261	59,985	64,318	206,610	155,182	140,455	197,320
Professional services	4,627	4,374	4,967	13,888	5,879	13,826	16,903
Attendance at juvenile programs							
In library	2,844	n.a.	1,381	2,658	783	1,522	1,677
Outside library	3,041	n.a.	1,738	5,898	1,887	1,855	388
Total	5,885	n.a.	3,119	8,556	2,670	3,337	2,065
Location							
Miles to nearest library	1.2	0.8	1.25	1.7	1.4	1.4	1.25
Miles to next nearest library	1.5	1.1	2.3	2.1	1.7	1.7	2.0
Accessibility [c]							
To elementary and secondary schools	110.3	108.9	38.4	5.5	7.7	6.1	8.9
To commercial areas	25.5	8.9	12.1	35.9	27.8	50.1	17.4

[a] Data provided by the Free Library of Philadelphia.
[b] Estimate of present capital value. See chapter 3.
[c] See Table 30.

The Individual Branch

area. Attendance at juvenile programs does not increase in this way.

To achieve a sufficiently large sample and a fairly good representation, the survey was carried on for two days in each library during March 1966—one weekday with evening hours and one Saturday. Both of these provide a reasonable coverage of adult use, which tends to be limited during weekday working hours. This means that the sample may not be representative of total use; however, the main purpose of the study was to determine how various groups in the community respond to the availability of library service. The possible sample bias does not conflict with this purpose.

Each visitor, as he entered the library, was handed a questionnaire stamped with his time of arrival. Survey personnel were available to help out with any questions, to collect the questionnaire when the visitor left, and to stamp the time of the departure. There were some refusals, some losses, and some unuseable answers, but the rate of return was, nevertheless, quite good. This can be seen in Table 9, in which, as in subsequent tables, libraries are arranged in order of the occupational level of the neighborhoods in which they are located.

Before carrying out the survey in the seven libraries, the questionnaire was tested in pilot interviews in the Cobbs Creek and the South Philadelphia branch libraries. The final questionnaire is presented as Figure 17.

The remainder of chapter 5 is devoted to a presentation of the basic data found in the survey. Data relating to characteristics of library users and use are presented first. They consist of:

1. Age of library users
2. Sex of library users
3. Occupation of library users

TABLE 9

Rate of Return of Useable Questionnaires

	Visitors (estimated number)	Questionnaires Returned and Useable	
		(number)	(percent)
Columbia	532	449	84.4
Richmond	471	400	84.9
Haddington	530	462	87.2
Frankford	1,548	1,125	72.7
Lovett	905	778	86.0
Wadsworth	1,032	759	73.5
Wynnefield	922	633	68.7

4. Purposes of visit to library
5. Use of services in the library
6. Use of other libraries by patrons of branches
7. Satisfaction of user

These are followed by data on travel patterns to libraries:

1. Distance of user's residence from library for all trips
2. Distance of user's residence from library for single-stop and multiple-stop trips
3. Means of transportation to libraries
4. Out-of-town users

Chapter 6 is more analytic in nature and focuses upon the effects of location on library use.

CHARACTERISTICS OF LIBRARY USERS AND USE

The use that is made of a facility and its services was shown earlier to be a function of the characteristics of the residents of its service area. The survey of seven libraries provides extensive

The Individual Branch 67

details on such characteristics as age, sex, and occupation of users.

Age of Library Users

Young people (eighteen years old and under) make up the majority of library users in each of the seven branches in the survey. (See Tables 10 and 11.) In the Columbia and Richmond branches, they constitute virtually all of the users—88 percent. This percentage is lower for the libraries in higher income areas. It is 64 percent for Lovett, 69 percent for Wadsworth, and 58 percent for Wynnefield. Young children (under fourteen years of age) by themselves constitute a majority in the three libraries in the lower income areas.

When the age structure of the population of each nominal service area is taken into account, the variation among libraries of the age of the user does not appear to be so large.[1] The relatively high rate of use by children and teen-agers can be seen in Table 11. In all cases, the percentage of users is well over twice as large as the percentage of residents in the child and teen-age categories. Rates of use by adults, on the other hand, are much lower. For adults, the percentage of users is usually considerably less than one-half the percentage of residents.

Sex of Library Users

More than half of all library users are female. The highest percentage observed is 66.0 percent of all users under fourteen years of age at Frankford; the lowest is 49.2 percent of all adults at Wynnefield (Table 12).

The predominance of females is most pronounced for persons under fourteen years of age. In this group, the percentage of females ranges between 59 percent and 66 percent. This probably should be expected, since young boys tend to favor active

FIGURE 17

Questionnaire Used in Branch Library Survey

[_] [_][_][_][_]   [_] [_][_][_][_][_]
 1   2 3 4   5   6 7 8 9 10

QUESTIONNAIRE

The Free Library is studying its services and their use as a basis for future planning and possible improvements. The questions below will take only a few minutes of your time. Please help us by completing this form and returning it at the desk before you leave. Thank you.

1. Address _____ [_][_]
                                                    12 13 14

2. Sex: Male ( ) Female ( )   [_]
                                                      16

3. Age   up to 5 ( )   10 to 13 ( )   19 to 25 ( )   46 to 65 ( )   [_][_]
         6 to 9 ( )   14 to 18 ( )   26 to 45 ( )   66 & over ( ) 17 18 19

4. a. Students through 12th Grade
   Name of School _____   [_][_]
   Father's Occupation _____   21 22
   Mother's Occupation: Housewife ( ) Other _____   [_] [_]
                                       (Specify)   23   24

   b. All Others (Please check below the item corresponding to your situation)
   Unemployed ( )
   Retired   ( )   [_][_]
                                                                    26 27
   Occupation _____
                (Specify)

5. Children under 14 years old.
   Did you come with a parent   ( )   another child ( )   [_]
                     a teacher ( )   alone   ( )   29
                     other adult ( )

6. Where did you come from ? (Only one check for your last stop)

    Home ( )   Public Facility (Playground, health center,
    Work ( )   post office...) (Specify) _____
    School ( )
    Shopping ( )   Other (Specify) _____ [ ]
                                                                             31

7. Where are you going upon leaving the library? (Only one check for your next stop)

    Home ( )   Public Facility...(playground, health center,
    Work ( )   post office...) (Specify) _____
    School ( )
    Shopping ( )   Other (Specify) _____ [ ]
                                                                             32

8. What means of transportation are you using on this library trip?

                                To Library   From Library
    Car   ( )   ( )
    PTC or Railroad   ( )   ( )   [ ] [ ]
    Walk, Bicycle   ( )   ( )   33 34

9. Is this the branch you usually use?   Yes ( )   No ( )   [ ]
                                                                             36

10. What other library facilities do you use?

    School Library   ( )   Other Branch _____
    College or University Library ( )   Other _____
    Northeast Regional   ( )   None ( )   [ ] [ ]
    Central (Logan Square) ( )   37 38

11. What were the purposes of your visit to the library today?

    Returning books   ( )   Business or professional ( )
    Reading for pleasure ( )   Personal Information   ( )   [ ]
    Student Assignment ( )   Other _____   40

12. While in the library today which of the following services did you use?

    Used books from open shelves   ( )   Attended program, book talk, meeting ( )
    Borrowed for use outside the library ( )   Other _____   [ ]
    Sought assistance from staff   ( )   None ( )   41

13. Have you any reason for dissatisfaction?

    Books wanted were out ( )   Librarian unable to answer questions ( )
    Too much noise   ( )   Parking difficulties   ( )
    No room to sit   ( )   Other _____   [ ]
    Limited selection   ( )   None ( )   43

sports and outside activities for their leisure time. For the teen-age group, the widest variation is observed: [2] a low of 46 percent females in Wadsworth and a high of 65 percent in Frankford. For adults, the variation is somewhat less, but only in Haddington and Wynnefield are females in the minority.

When the sex distribution of the population is taken into account (Table 12), the preponderance of female library users is not quite so pervasive. In the adult group, males are over-represented among users of four of the seven libraries. In the child and teen-age groups, however, females are found to be in substantially greater proportion as library users than they are in the population itself. The only exceptions are teen-agers in Wadsworth and Wynnefield. These areas are of upper socio-economic level and are predominantly Jewish—meaning that they contain a cultural group that tends to accord more than average prestige to intellectual activities for boys.

Occupations of Library Users

Libraries tend to be much more heavily used by white-collar workers than by blue-collar workers. (See Table 13.) The children of blue-collar workers, however, use the library much more than do adult blue-collar workers.[3] This indicates that the libraries may be fulfilling their goals of increasing equality of opportunity and cultural integration.

Although some of the children in low-income areas may be taking advantage of their opportunities to improve their education and their potential for economic and personal success, they still represent a small proportion of low-income children. Many more children in high-income areas are taking advantage of these opportunities.

In particular, the percentage of library users employed as pro-

TABLE 10

Age and Sex of Library Users

	Male	Female	No Answer	Total
Columbia				
Under 14	101	152	28	281
14-18	41	72	2	115
Over 18	21	31	1	53
Total	163	255	31	449
Richmond				
Under 14	68	117	22	207
14-18	55	88	3	146
Over 18	23	24	0	47
Total	146	229	25	400
Haddington				
Under 14	77	147	21	245
14-18	61	62	2	125
Over 18	47	45	0	92
Total	185	254	23	462
Frankford				
Under 14	109	208	14	331
14-18	150	272	2	424
Over 18	170	189	11	370
Total	429	669	27	1125
Lovett				
Under 14	93	147	22	262
14-18	55	96	1	152
Over 18	170	187	7	364
Total	318	430	30	778
Wadsworth				
Under 14	112	167	12	291
14-18	124	109	2	235
Over 18	104	129	0	233
Total	340	405	14	759
Wynnefield				
Under 14	60	85	4	149
14-18	110	105	5	220
Over 18	127	130	7	264
Total	297	320	16	633

TABLE 11

Age of Library Users

	Percent of Total Users			Ratio of Percent of Users to Percent of Residents		
	Under 14	14-18	Over 18	Under 14	14-18	Over 18
Columbia	62.0	26.1	11.9	2.8	2.4	0.18
Richmond	51.3	36.8	11.9	3.8	4.3	0.15
Haddington	52.8	27.1	20.1	3.7	3.1	0.26
Frankford	29.0	37.2	33.8	1.9	4.4	0.44
Lovett	33.3	19.5	47.2	2.6	2.5	0.60
Wadsworth	38.2	31.1	30.7	2.5	3.3	0.41
Wynnefield	23.6	34.6	41.8	2.0	5.1	0.52

TABLE 12

Sex of Library Users

	Percent of Female Users			Ratio of Percent of Female Users to Percent of Female Residents		
	Under 14	14-18 in Secondary School	Adults	Under 14	14-18 in Secondary School	Adults
Columbia	60.0	63.1	61.5	1.10	1.29	1.12
Richmond	63.0	60.9	53.7	1.27	1.24	1.04
Haddington	60.0	50.4	48.5	1.20	1.08	0.88
Frankford	66.0	65.0	52.7	1.34	1.33	0.92
Lovett	62.0	63.3	52.0	1.23	1.30	0.93
Wadsworth	59.8	45.8	55.8	1.24	0.93	1.02
Wynnefield	57.0	47.7	49.2	1.14	0.96	0.88

fessionals, managers, or officials is much higher than the percentage of these occupations in the population as a whole. This finding confirms the observation made in the analysis of chapter 4 that library use is much heavier among higher income groups.

Purposes of the Library Visit

There do not seem to be any major differences among branches in reasons for trips to the library. (See Table 14.) This finding strengthens our assumption that all branches can be regarded as comparable units performing similar functions and that additional branches are added to the system in order to make library service more accessible or convenient to users, rather than to add new types of service.

Among adults, "reading for pleasure" was the purpose most frequently checked (30 percent to 38 percent in the various libraries). The second most frequent was "personal information" (12 percent to 20 percent). "Business or professional" was relatively unimportant (3.4 percent to 9.2 percent).

For young children, also, "reading for pleasure" was the major purpose of library visits (33 percent to 48 percent).

TABLE 13

Occupation of Adult Library Users and of Parents of Child Library Users
(in percent)

	Columbia	Richmond	Haddington	Frankford	Lovett	Wadsworth	Wynnefield
Adults							
Professionals, managers, officials[a]	23.5	6.1	48.0	33.7	69.4	60.9	64.9
Population[b]	4.9	8.6	11.6	16.0	36.4	41.2	41.8
Clerical, sales-service	44.1	56.6	30.8	43.7	21.1	27.8	29.8
Craftsmen, operatives	14.7	27.3	21.2	22.1	9.5	10.4	5.3
Laborers	17.3	10.0		0.5		0.9	
Children: Father's occupation							
Professionals, managers, officials	6.6	5.9	24.4	24.2	44.3	47.3	58.0
Clerical, sales-service	22.5	20.4	22.2	19.8	24.2	34.8	23.4
Craftsmen, operatives	57.2	57.7	51.8	52.7	29.2	16.6	15.1
Laborers	13.7	16.0	2.6	3.3	2.3	1.3	3.5
Children: Mother's occupation[c]							
Professionals, managers, officials	21.2	1.8	25.0	16.2	47.4	37.2	48.8
Clerical, sales-service	22.4	50.0	41.7	60.5	43.8	61.0	47.7
Craftsmen, operatives	20.0	12.5	33.3	22.2	7.1	1.8	4.5
Laborers	36.4	37.7		1.1	1.7		

Note: Blank cells signify 0, or less than 0.01 percent.
[a]Data from U.S. Census of Population: 1960.
[b]Ibid. Note that, unlike all other percentages in this table, which are of library users, these percentages are of the total population in the service area.
[c]When employed.

TABLE 14

Purpose of Library Visit
(in percent)

	Columbia	Richmond	Haddington	Frankford	Lovett	Wadsworth	Wynnefield
Children under 14							
Reading for pleasure	40.3	34.7	33.6	35.9	45.6	48.2	39.9
Student assignment	18.3	20.0	30.3	23.0	23.2	25.8	38.6
Returning books	31.3	45.0	38.1	46.0	53.3	35.8	35.8
Other	20.2	3.8	10.7	12.6	7.7	11.0	21.6
No answer	7.5	2.4	2.0	0.3	0.8	4.1	2.7
Persons over 14 in secondary school							
Reading for pleasure	25.6	28.4	17.7	22.2	28.6	19.6	18.4
Student assignment	46.9	51.1	63.9	56.5	57.1	56.4	71.7
Returning books	29.2	39.0	39.6	33.0	46.2	27.3	31.6
Other	20.3	12.8	8.4	7.1	7.5	24.1	16.1
No answer	1.8	0.7	0.8	1.2		1.8	3.7
Adults							
Reading for pleasure	37.9	37.0	31.4	36.8	38.2	38.2	30.2
Business or profession	3.4	7.4	5.5	5.6	7.8	9.2	6.4
Personal information	18.9	18.5	14.1	12.5	20.4	16.1	20.2
Returning books	44.8	31.5	43.5	51.0	56.2	43.8	43.7
Other	25.8	24.1	29.3	15.4	17.2	20.9	31.9
No answer	5.2		1.0	1.8	1.6	0.8	1.3

Note: Blank cells signify 0, or less than 0.01 percent.

"Student assignments" ran second (18.3 percent to 38.6 percent).

For teen-agers (children over fourteen), a different pattern is evident. "Student assignment" was by far the major purpose of library visits. It was indicated by between 47 percent and 72 percent of respondents—percentages two to three times those for "reading for pleasure."

The purpose receiving the largest number of responses was "returning books"; however, the books returned may have been those read for pleasure, for student assignment, for business and professional, or for other reasons.[4]

Use of Services in the Library

Use of open-shelf material (reported by 35 percent to 53 percent of library users) and borrowing for use outside the library (reported by 30 percent to 50 percent of library users) are the most important services, as shown in Table 15.

Preliminary cross-tabulations indicated that *never* is any other service used without an accompanying use of books from the open shelves. The specific cross-tabulations indicate that a rather large number of open-shelf users neither borrowed books nor sought assistance from the staff. Of the remaining open-shelf users, there are two groups: a very small one of individuals who both borrowed books and sought assistance from the staff and a much larger one of individuals who only borrowed books or only sought assistance. (See Table 16.)

The fact that large numbers of individuals who sought assistance did not borrow books suggests that the number of professional services offered is an important part of the output of a library and that this figure may not be adequately subsumed by circulation.

If the number of users who seek assistance only is added to

TABLE 15

Services Used in the Library
(in percent)

	Columbia	Richmond	Haddington	Frankford	Lovett	Wadsworth	Wynnefield
Children under 14							
Open shelves	41.4	38.1	42.3	43.2	40.2	46.2	52.7
Outside circulation	31.3	31.2	33.2	35.6	64.8	32.8	44.9
Assistance from staff	3.6	6.8	14.3	8.9	9.3	15.2	16.9
Other	9.0	2.9	2.9	1.2	0.3	2.1	6.8
No answer	7.9	3.9	5.3	2.4	3.5	3.8	4.1
None	13.3	23.4	13.1	21.2	15.5	15.5	8.1
Persons over 14 in secondary school							
Open shelves	42.5	49.7	35.3	39.6	41.5	40.9	49.2
Outside circulation	31.8	34.8	46.2	34.0	36.1	31.8	39.6
Assistance from staff	7.1	12.1	17.6	17.1	14.3	19.5	20.8
Other	3.5	1.4	2.5	2.1	6.8	9.5	6.4
No answer	9.7	2.8	3.4	2.7	6.8	5.4	4.3
None	12.4	12.8	12.6	18.8	21.1	20.4	11.7
Adults							
Open shelves	53.5	50.0	47.5	43.9	38.7	40.2	45.6
Outside circulation	34.4	31.4	34.4	37.9	48.6	43.0	50.3
Assistance from staff	15.5	5.5	14.3	10.5	9.9	14.8	13.8
Other	3.4		6.6	2.0	1.6	2.0	4.4
No answer	6.9	5.5	6.6	7.2	6.7	4.8	3.0
None	5.2	11.1	14.2	13.6	10.0	12.8	7.7

TABLE 16

Borrowing for Use Outside Library vs. Use of Assistance from Staff
(in numbers)

	Children under 14		Over 14 in Secondary School		Adults		Total	
	Borrowed	Did Not Borrow	Borrowed	Did Not Borrow	Borrowed	Did Not Borrow	Borrowed	Did Not Borrow
Columbia								
Assistance	15	72	6	30	4	16	25	118
No assistance	100	69	42	24	27	7	169	90
Richmond								
Assistance	2	62	10	39	1	15	13	116
No assistance	76	57	60	28	26	9	162	94
Haddington								
Assistance	10	71	8	47	8	26	26	144
No assistance	93	57	34	25	39	20	166	102
Frankford								
Assistance	24	92	22	117	31	117	77	226
No assistance	117	85	140	119	140	74	397	278
Lovett								
Assistance	22	94	17	36	31	150	70	280
No assistance	82	52	44	44	113	53	237	107
Wadsworth								
Assistance	20	75	31	39	16	91	67	205
No assistance	114	70	59	79	84	46	257	195
Wynnefield								
Assistance	25	40	26	48	42	108	93	196
No assistance	53	24	66	39	94	45	213	108

the number of users who borrow books (whether they seek assistance or not), the total number of users is 60 percent to 75 percent larger than the number of borrowers alone for five of the seven libraries. (See the last column of Table 17.) For Frankford, this number is only 48 percent larger than the number of borrowers, and for Lovett it is 90 percent larger. The rankings of the surveyed libraries based on total number of users would be substantially the same as that based on number of borrowers alone. Nevertheless, the difference in the measure of output based on total users, as opposed to borrowers only (or book circulation), might be significant in library system planning.[5]

Use of Other Libraries by Branch Patrons

Data on distance from residence to the branch library, which is presented later, describe most of the trips related to the library system. Although most persons interviewed normally use a given branch, a large number of trips are made to other branches, to school libraries, to the Northwest Regional Library, and to the central library. (See Table 18.)

The dependence of the library user on a particular branch is shown by the fact that at the various libraries at least 82.3 percent (and up to 91.5 percent) of those interviewed stated that they usually used that branch. At least 16 percent (and up to 38 percent) of all adults stated that they did not use any other branch.

The degree of absolute dependence upon the local branch library appears to be greatest for users in neighborhoods of low-income levels, where people presumably have relatively low mobility and a restricted scope of information. In communities where the socioeconomic level is high—the vicinity of the Lovett

TABLE 17

Individuals Borrowing and Seeking Assistance from Staff

	Borrowing and assistance (percent)	Borrowing only (percent) (number)		Assistance only (percent) (number)		Total Users[a] (percent) (number)		Ratio of Total Users to Total Borrowers
Columbia	8.0	54.2	195	37.8	118	100	313	1.60
Richmond	4.2	55.8	175	40.0	116	100	291	1.66
Haddington	7.7	49.5	192	42.8	144	100	336	1.75
Frankford	11.0	56.7	474	32.3	226	100	700	1.48
Lovett	11.9	40.5	307	47.6	280	100	587	1.91
Wadsworth	12.8	48.5	324	38.7	205	100	529	1.63
Wynnefield	18.5	42.5	306	39.0	195	100	502	1.64

[a] Sum of individuals who borrow and seek assistance and those who borrow only.

and Wadsworth branches, for example—there appears to be less dependence on a single branch library. The limited use of other branches by adult patrons of the Wynnefield branch may be explained by the fact that there are no branches in nearby neighborhoods of comparable socioeconomic level.

The amount of use made of other branches is of particular interest in the study of service areas. Those persons using more than one branch are contributors to the overlap of service areas. They range from 2 percent to 39 percent of all adults interviewed in the various libraries. The other component of overlap consists of marginal areas—a block for example—where some residents use one library exclusively and some use another. The relative importance of the two components of overlap is studied in chapter 5.

The use of the central or regional library is predictably low for young branch library users, but these facilities are used by between one-half and three-quarters of the high school students who use the branch libraries. Distance to the central or regional library does not appear to affect these proportions. For adults, the percentage using the central or regional library is generally even higher (30 percent to 50 percent of adults). It should be

TABLE 18

Branch Patrons' Use of Other Libraries
(in percent)

	Columbia	Richmond	Haddington	Frankford	Lovett	Wadsworth	Wynnefield
Total normally using library[a]	88.6	91.5	86.6	84.1	85.5	83.7	82.3
Children under 14							
No other library	43.5	45.0	48.8	36.2	24.0	12.8	13.5
Another branch	1.1	1.0	6.1	8.6	9.6	15.5	6.1
School library	45.0	46.0	42.0	51.0	66.0	79.0	77.0
Pupils in parochial schools[b]	17.0	75.0	79.0	61.0	27.0	9.0	13.0
Persons over 14 in secondary school							
No other library	11.0	6.0	20.0	13.0	5.0	9.0	5.0
Another branch	3.0	9.0	11.0	10.0	21.0	32.0	11.0
Central and/or regional library	24.0	44.0	35.0	39.0	32.0	55.0	58.0
School library	81.0	70.0	56.0	72.0	84.0	81.0	67.0
Adults							
No other library	36.0	33.0	33.0	38.0	22.0	16.0	22.0
Another branch	2.0	6.0	22.0	14.0	28.0	39.0	13.0
Central and/or regional library	40.0	50.0	27.0	37.0	34.0	39.0	49.0

[a] Total replying yes to question 9: "Is this the library you usually use?"
[b] Refers to percent of respondents who attend parochial schools rather than to percent of respondents using libraries.

The Individual Branch 79

emphasized that there is no information on the frequency of use and that some users may have been only once to one of these other libraries.

Children have access to a particular facility—their school libraries. At the high school level (over fourteen years old), the percentage of children using their school library is very high (between 56 percent and 84 percent). Relatively low use of school libraries was reported by patrons of the Wynnefield and, particularly, of the Haddington branches.

At the elementary or junior high school level (persons under fourteen years old), less use of school libraries is reported. Table 18 also presents the distribution of the children with respect to the kind of schools they attend—parochial versus public or private. The larger the proportion of users who attend parochial schools, the smaller the percentage who report using school library facilities. This relationship appears for users of all branches but Columbia.

Since the time of this survey (spring 1966), libraries in the Philadelphia public schools have been enlarged and expanded. It is possible that a new survey would indicate a higher use of school libraries and a relatively lower use of branch community libraries, particularly for purposes related to children's school work.

Satisfaction of User [6]

Roughly half the child and adult users found no reason for dissatisfaction with the library facilities and services provided. (See Table 19.) For children under fourteen, the percentage finding no reason for dissatisfaction ranged between 45.2 percent and 64.7 percent for the various libraries. For adults, the range was between 43.8 percent and 63.6 percent.

Teen-agers were more highly critical. Only at Richmond did

a majority find no reason for dissatisfaction. For the various libraries, the percentage of teen-agers finding no dissatisfaction ranged from 32.7 percent to 51.8 percent.

For all groups, the major complaints were the two related items "books were out" and "limited selection." "Books were out" tends to be cited more frequently by younger users and "limited selection" by older users. Taken together, they were cited by between 17.8 percent and 31.4 percent of persons under fourteen using the various libraries, by between 28.2 percent and 56.8 percent of the persons over fourteen in secondary school, and by between 24.1 percent and 37.9 percent of the adults.

For adults and secondary school students, these responses appear to be related to social class: the higher the social class, the higher the percentage of those finding books out or selection inadequate. The responses also appear to be related to the pressure on the bookstock, as measured by the average annual number of borrowings per book (annual circulation divided by bookstock). The responses, therefore, seem to reflect the actual situation: heavy book demand leads to requests for a wide variety of books and to the high probability of books being out.

These responses do not justify the conclusion that the low rate of use in low-income areas is caused by limited or unsuitable bookstock. It is true, as noted in Table 8, that bookstock in libraries serving low-income areas tends to be substantially smaller than in libraries serving high-income areas. But both the circulation per book and dissatisfaction are low in low-income areas. One should not conclude from this analysis, however, that it is useless to improve bookstock for the purpose of attracting more users in low-income areas.

One suggestive finding from the survey is that, in low-income

TABLE 19

Reasons for Dissatisfaction with Library Service
(in percent)

	Columbia	Richmond	Haddington	Frankford	Lovett	Wadsworth	Wynnefield
Children under 14							
None	47.4	54.5	53.7	64.7	56.0	48.6	45.2
Books were out	17.3	16.6	17.2	12.0	20.8	19.0	20.1
Limited selection	9.0	7.3	7.0	5.8	6.9	12.4	5.4
Noise	20.1	18.5	6.6	8.9	6.6	13.4	6.1
No room to sit	4.7	6.8	3.7	8.0	4.6	9.3	2.7
Librarian unable to help	1.4	2.9	2.0	0.3	0.8	3.8	2.0
Parking difficulties		0.4		2.4	1.2	1.4	2.7
Other	0.4	0.4	5.3	3.7	2.3	5.9	12.8
No answer	12.6	3.9	11.5	4.9	7.7	8.3	13.5
Four or more answers	1.1	2.9		1.5	0.5	2.1	1.4
Persons over 14 in secondary school							
None	43.4	51.8	42.0	42.2	46.3	32.7	39.5
Books were out	17.7	14.9	26.1	20.5	27.9	28.6	25.6
Limited selection	11.5	23.4	20.2	15.4	21.1	28.2	30.4
Noise	15.1	8.5	6.7	6.1	6.8	11.8	3.2
No room to sit	9.7	1.4	3.4	18.1	4.1	9.5	
Librarian unable to help		4.3	4.2	1.5		2.7	1.1
Parking difficulties	1.8	2.1	2.5	6.4	27.2	7.7	9.1
Other	4.4	0.7	2.5	5.6	4.8	12.7	7.5
No answer	10.6	7.1	10.9	8.1	7.5	6.4	5.3
Four or more answers	0.9	0.7	4.0	1.7	0.7	4.1	1.6
Adults							
None	60.4	61.1	63.6	55.8	54.3	43.8	47.3
Books were out	10.3	5.6	12.1	9.5	11.5	12.8	14.4
Limited selection	13.8	18.5	12.1	13.1	16.4	21.3	23.5
Noise	5.2	5.6	1.0	3.8	4.3	14.1	4.0
No room to sit				2.0	1.3		13.4
Librarian unable to help	3.4		1.0			1.2	
Parking difficulties	3.4		2.0	10.5	4.3	1.1	14.1
Other	3.4	7.4	1.0	2.6	5.1	3.2	6.0
No answer	13.8	7.4	12.1	11.3	11.0	10.4	7.7
Four or more answers	1.7					0.4	0.7
Measures of pressure on capacity							
Average number of times book borrowed per year	1.7	2.9	2.7	4.0	3.9	3.6	4.1
Users per square foot [a]	0.062	0.049	0.065	0.13	0.11	0.17	0.073
Crowding index [b]	17.6	9.6	15.7	67.1	44.4	66.8	34.6

Note: Blank cells indicate less than 0.01 percent.

[a] Users are the number of visitors during the survey period.
[b] Users x Bookstock/square feet of floorspace x 10^2.

areas, the percentage of users who mentioned no dissatisfaction fell more slowly from the child to the teen-age categories and rose more rapidly from the teen-age to the adult categories than it did in upper-income areas. This suggests that in the low-income areas the younger users are relatively more demanding. The heavy demand by the young in all areas may be explained by the pressure of homework assignments that require particular books. But the relative lack of dissatisfaction of the older users in low-income areas may be best explained by their relatively low educational levels, which could lead to less discrimination in their borrowing. If their children, who are getting educational experiences and schooling well beyond that of their parents, remain in their neighborhoods, it is likely that adult demands will increase relatively over the years. This suggests the desirability of a program of bookstock acquisition in such areas that will continue to meet the needs of an increasingly educated population, thereby increasing the attraction of the library to adults. Such a conclusion is also supported by Table 11, which indicates that the ratio of young to adult users is substantially higher in low-income areas than in areas of higher income and educational achievement.

Inadequate professional help does not appear to be a major problem in the opinion of the users, but quiet, traditionally the essence of the library environment, does appear to be quite important. In the various libraries, complaints of excessive noise were made by 6.1 percent to 20.1 percent of the children under fourteen, by 3.2 percent to 15.1 percent of the persons over fourteen in secondary school, and by 1.0 percent to 14.1 percent of the adults. Complaints about noise were significantly higher in Columbia and Richmond than in all other libraries except Wadsworth. The problem of noise in Wadsworth may be explained by the library's crowded conditions, which is reflected both in the complaints about lack of seating space and the fact of limited space per user. Columbia and Richmond have a relatively large amount of floor space per user, so the noise complaints may have to be explained by the behavioral characteristics of the users or by the acoustical design deficiencies of the library buildings. The existence of noise may well provide a partial explanation for the low use rates of these two libraries. It may also suggest the need for special consideration of interior design to reduce noise in libraries in low-income areas.

Lack of seating space was a problem in the various libraries for 3.7 percent to 9.3 percent of the children under fourteen, for up to 18.1 percent of persons over fourteen in secondary school, and for up to 13.4 percent of the adults. Adults found lack of seating space a problem in only three libraries. The complaints about lack of seating space seem reasonable in light of pressure on space caused by both users and bookstock. The highest percentage of complaints came from those libraries (especially Frankford and Wadsworth) where the users per square foot and users times books per square foot is the largest. Furthermore, there is no indication in either the survey responses or the measures of space congestion that low rates of use in low-income areas are caused by crowding in the library.

Parking difficulty, the only complaint relating directly to the location of the library, was cited infrequently. Parking appears to be a major difficulty only at Lovett and Wynnefield. However, these responses are not very consistent, since, at Lovett, 27.2 percent of teen-agers but only 4.3 percent of adults found it a problem. At Wynnefield, on the other hand, parking was a difficulty for only 7.7 percent of the teen-agers and for 14.1 percent of the adults.

CHARACTERISTICS OF TRAVEL TO THE LIBRARY

The pattern of users' residences has been studied for the seven libraries surveyed. Curves of cumulative percentages showing increasing distance of all users from the library are presented in Figures 18 through 24. The data are given in Table 20. The figures are arranged in order of increasing size of apparent market area. They begin with Richmond, 98 percent of whose young users and 88 percent of whose adult users live within three-fourths of a mile of the library.

For Wynnefield, the library with the second largest market area, a distance of two miles is reached before 88 percent of the children and 70 percent of the adults are accounted for. Frankford, the library with the largest market area, appears to be an anomaly: whereas the curves of most of the libraries rise quickly over a relatively short distance and then flatten out, the curves for Frankford rise more slowly and steadily throughout a distance of one mile.

In the figures, separate curves are given for four age classes (up to nine, ten to thirteen, over fourteen in high school, and adult). The locations of the nearest and the next nearest library are also plotted on each of the figures. All distances are measured along streets.

Distance of User's Residence from the Library for Single-stop and Multistop Trips

In the case of a library located in a commercial area, one might suppose that library users would combine stops at some commercial facilities with their trip to the library. Since several purposes can be served by such a trip, it is reasonable to suppose

The Individual Branch

that such users would be willing to travel a longer distance from home to the library than would users for whom a stop at the library was the sole purpose of the trip. In general, the survey data bear out these suppositions. Data on previous stops and subsequent stops by library users are given in Table 21.

The *home* of the library user is the origin or termination of much more than one-half of the library trips for both children and adults. In some cases—Richmond, for example—the proportion of library trips with home as one other stop is as high as nine out of ten.[7] It can be seen from Table 21, in which libraries are arranged according to increasing average distance from home to library, that, in general, as average distance increases, the proportion of home trips decreases. It may be inferred that as residents from a greater and greater distance use the library, they do so because they are able to combine stops at the library with trips to work, shopping, or school.

Next to "home," shopping is the stop most frequently associated with a library visit—for both children and for adults. Table 21 indicates a strong relationship between accessibility of commercial area and proportion of library users who indicate their last stop or next stop to be "shopping." The only library that does not fit the relationship well is Columbia, which is actually separated from its commercial area by Ridge Avenue. This correlation and the measurement of accessibility to commercial activity is discussed more fully in chapter 6.

As might be expected, work for adults and school for children are sometimes associated with visits to the library. Looking at the detailed results, the patterns of linked trips such as work–library–home or school–library–home are quite apparent. The percentage of trips involving school appears to bear no simple relation to the accessibility of schools to the library.

Finally, the number of stops at public facilities is very in-

TABLE 20

Library Users Responding to Survey, by Distance

Miles from Library	Up to 9 Years	10-13 Years	Over 14, in Secondary School	Adults
		Columbia		
Less than 1/8	9	3	2	4
Less than 1/4	26	43	27	10
Less than 3/8	51	74	63	24
Less than 1/2	75	118	82	32
Less than 5/8	85	143	91	37
Less than 3/4	90	167	104	43
Less than 7/8	92	171	104	46
Less than 1	92	178	108	47
Less than 1 1/4	92	179	109	49
Less than 1 1/2	92	180	110	50
Less than 2	92	180	111	53
2 and over	93	183	112	53
No answer	1	1	1	5
		Frankford		
Less than 1/8	1	1	3	9
Less than 1/4	4	12	12	33
Less than 3/8	6	31	25	62
Less than 1/2	15	70	64	97
Less than 5/8	25	94	109	123
Less than 3/4	32	109	137	150
Less than 7/8	42	136	182	182
Less than 1	47	158	211	207
Less than 1 1/4	68	194	293	259
Less than 1 1/2	76	228	347	294
Less than 2	80	231	382	313
2 and over	82	240	400	363
No answer	1	3	9	27
		Haddington		
Less than 1/8	15	35	23	3
Less than 1/4	29	66	40	12
Less than 3/8	49	96	57	24
Less than 1/2	63	121	72	33
Less than 5/8	67	148	88	42
Less than 3/4	69	161	94	54
Less than 7/8	71	164	99	64
Less than 1	71	165	107	68
Less than 1 1/4	72	165	113	78
Less than 1 1/2	72	167	114	82
Less than 2	72	170	114	84
2 and over	72	170	118	93
No answer	0	0	1	6
		Lovett		
Less than 1/8	3	1	1	4
Less than 1/4	18	25	23	34
Less than 3/8	42	52	41	77
Less than 1/2	58	76	63	119
Less than 5/8	72	115	88	165
Less than 3/4	80	130	100	198
Less than 7/8	89	139	113	236
Less than 1	93	141	116	257
Less than 1 1/4	95	147	119	290
Less than 1 1/2	95	150	122	307
Less than 2	96	151	129	324
2 and over	99	156	143	357
No answer	2	2	4	15

Miles from Library	Up to 9 Years	10-13 Years	Over 14, in Secondary School	Adults
		Richmond		
Less than 1/8	17	35	23	10
Less than 1/4	40	60	55	23
Less than 3/8	62	80	81	37
Less than 1/2	79	106	100	41
Less than 5/8	72	118	116	44
Less than 3/4	73	120	121	46
Less than 7/8	73	123	128	47
Less than 1	73	124	131	47
Less than 1 1/4	73	125	133	47
Less than 1 1/2	75	125	133	47
Less than 2	75	125	133	47
2 and over	75	125	135	50
No answer	2	3	3	4
		Wadsworth		
Less than 1/8	12	29	18	19
Less than 1/4	24	80	54	58
Less than 3/8	38	132	82	92
Less than 1/2	43	144	99	106
Less than 5/8	48	166	123	122
Less than 3/4	49	173	134	130
Less than 7/8	53	186	140	140
Less than 1	56	189	151	149
Less than 1 1/4	59	197	157	164
Less than 1 1/2	60	200	169	179
Less than 2	62	204	184	202
2 and over	66	220	213	245
No answer	1	3	7	4
		Wynnefield		
Less than 1/8	1	2	4	5
Less than 1/4	1	6	7	19
Less than 3/8	4	15	16	27
Less than 1/2	13	34	24	58
Less than 5/8	19	48	47	81
Less than 3/4	20	67	76	115
Less than 7/8	22	75	90	134
Less than 1	23	78	96	153
Less than 1 1/4	25	82	98	162
Less than 1 1/2	26	85	106	181
Less than 2	29	89	120	193
2 and over	33	106	178	277
No answer	3	7	9	21

KEY FOR FIGURES 18-24:

― ― ― ―   Up to 9 Years Old

―·―··―·―   10 - 13 Years Old

♦♦♦♦♦♦♦   Over 14 Years Old
in Secondary School

―――――   Adults

―■―――   Nearest Library

―■―――   Next Nearest Library

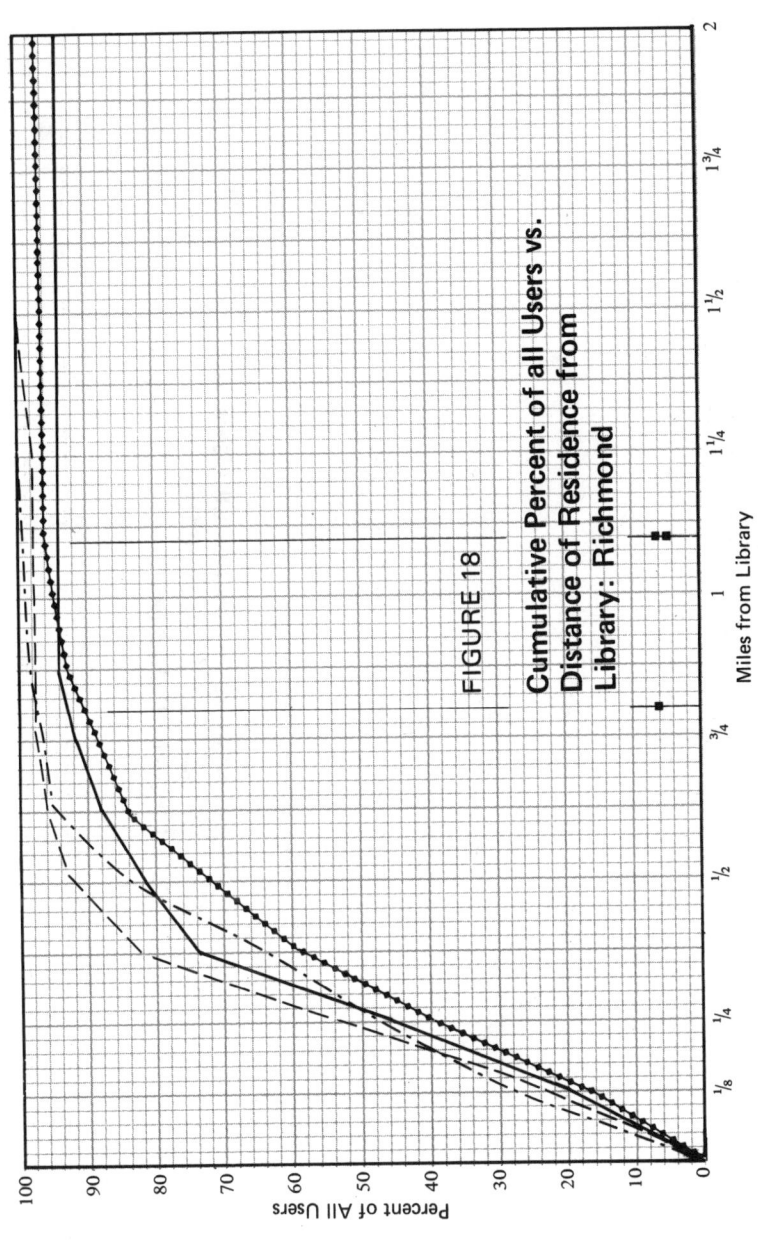

FIGURE 18

Cumulative Percent of all Users vs. Distance of Residence from Library: Richmond

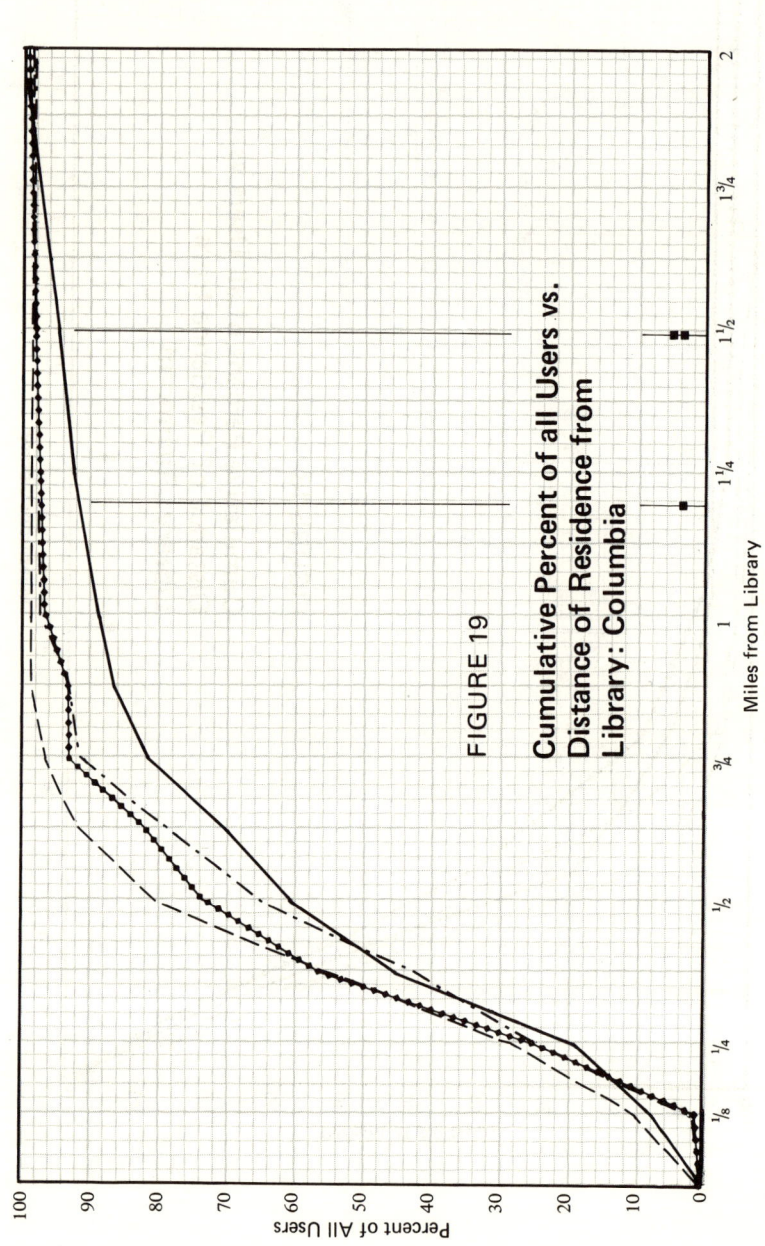

FIGURE 19

Cumulative Percent of all Users vs. Distance of Residence from Library: Columbia

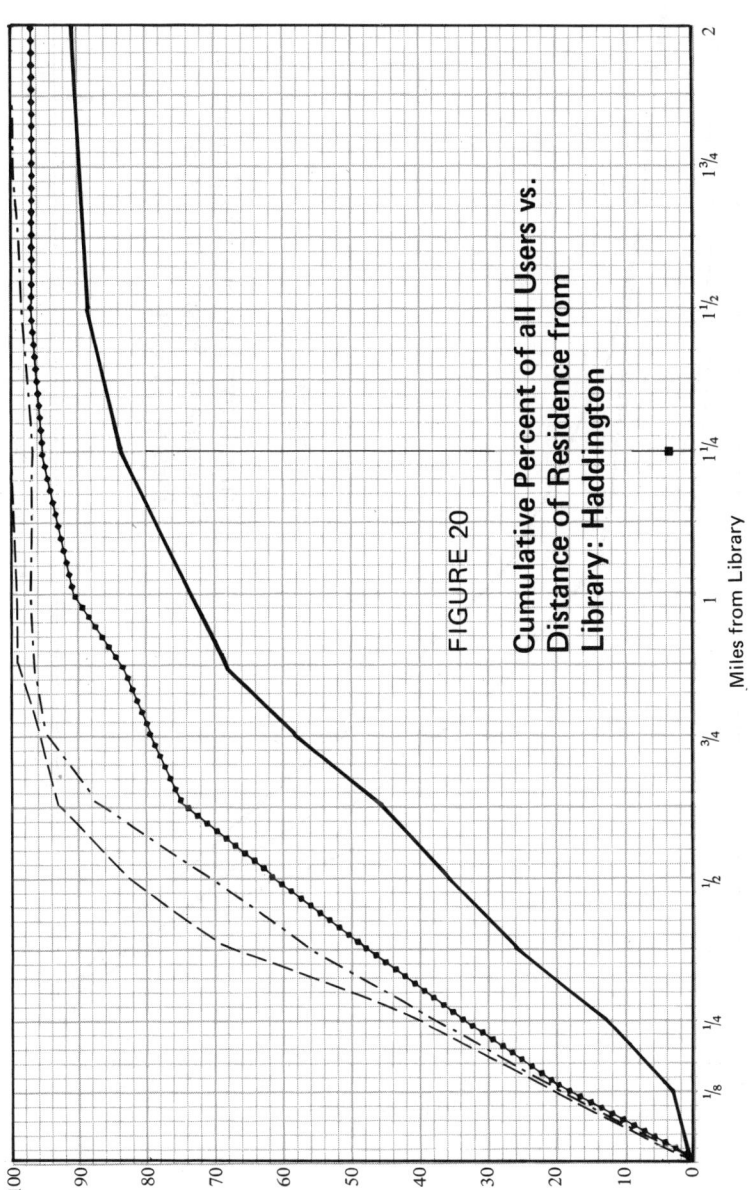

FIGURE 20

Cumulative Percent of all Users vs. Distance of Residence from Library: Haddington

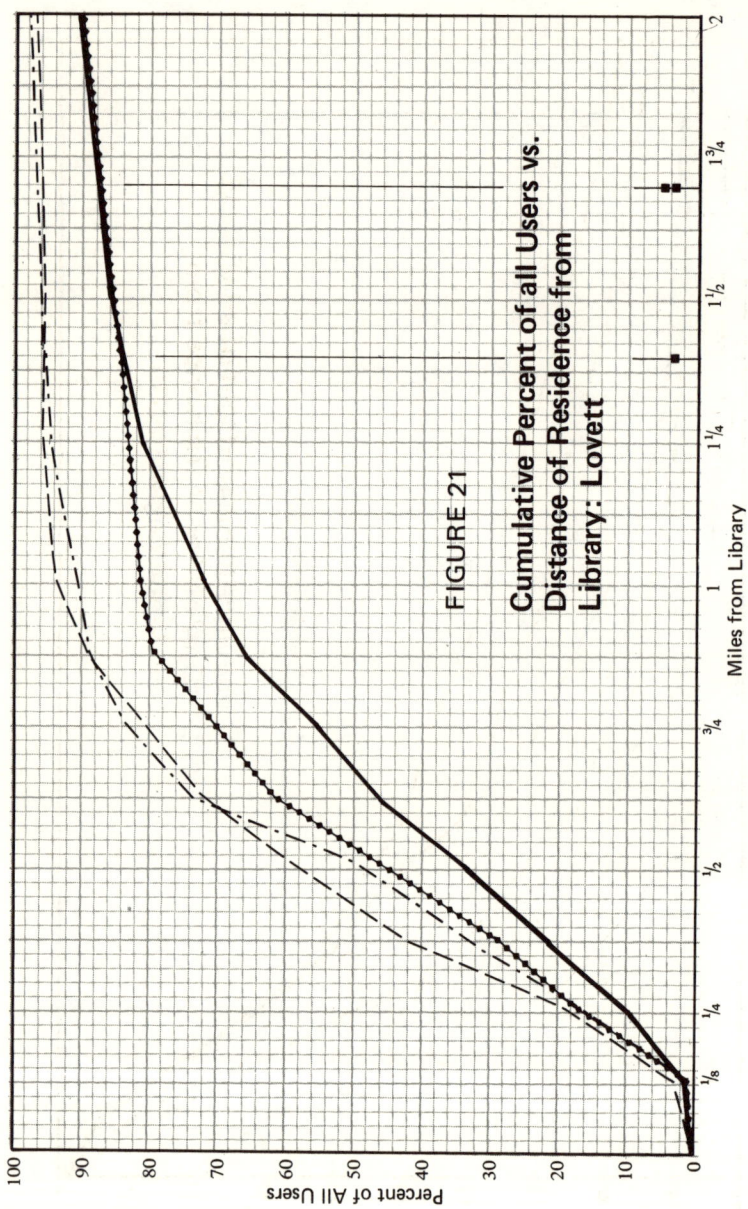

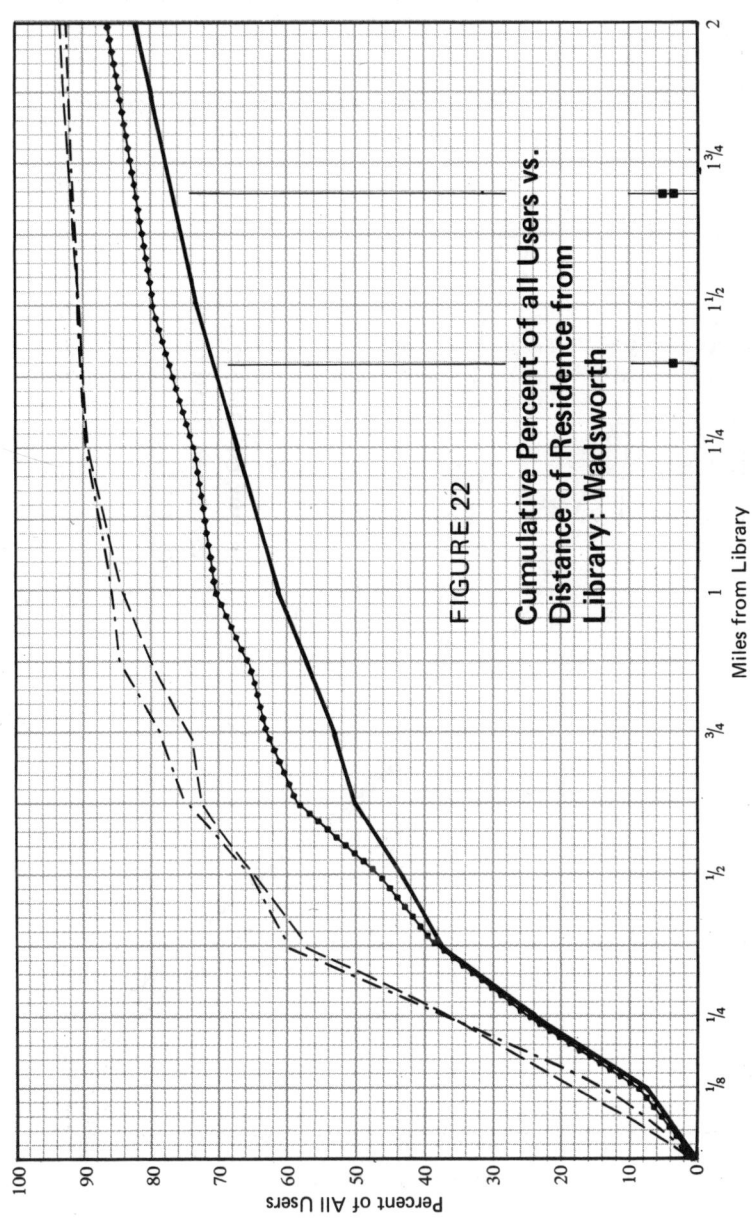

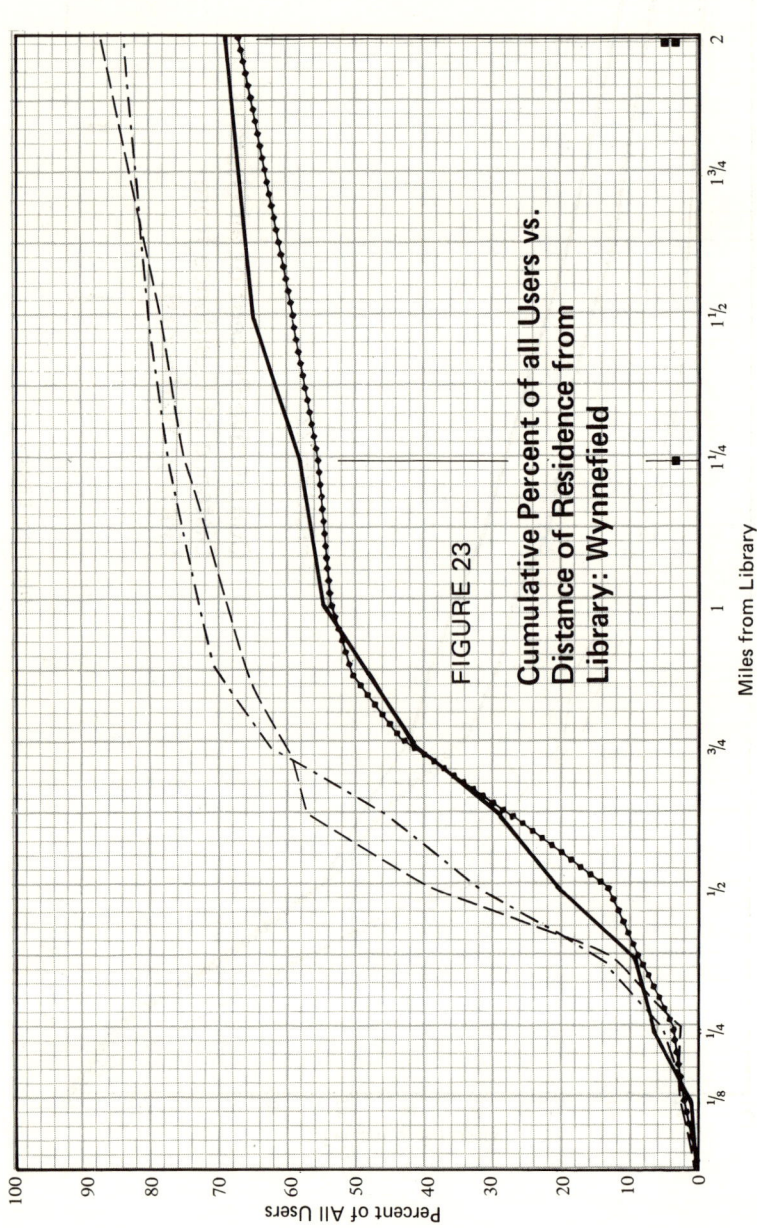

FIGURE 23
Cumulative Percent of all Users vs. Distance of Residence from Library: Wynnefield

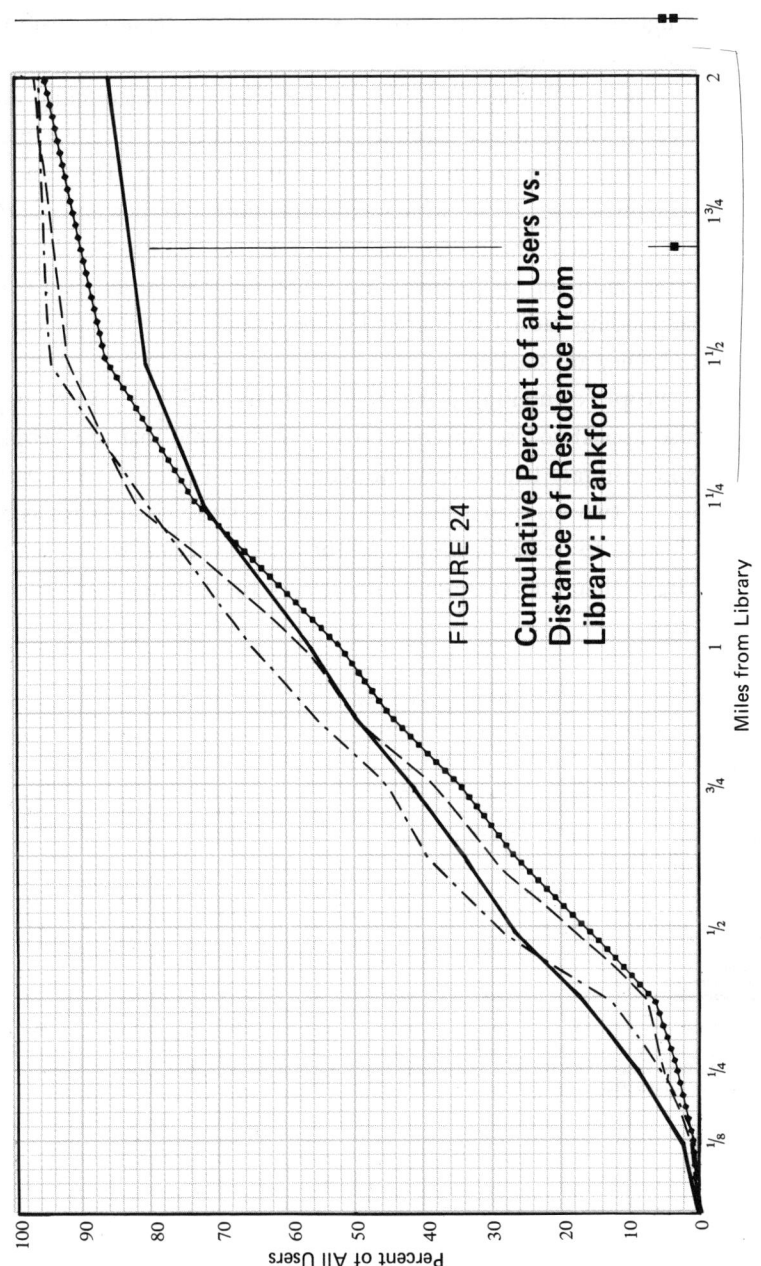

FIGURE 24

Cumulative Percent of all Users vs. Distance of Residence from Library: Frankford

significant. The only cases worth reporting are those of Haddington and Richmond, where some children reported visiting the nearby playground.

People who combine a trip to the library with shopping are clearly willing to use a library farther from home than are persons who make no other stops on their library trip. This can be seen in Table 22 in which radii including 80 percent of all trips to each library are shown for three age groups. In ten cases, radii for "trips involving shopping" are larger than corresponding radii for "home–library–home" trips; in two cases only they are smaller.

People combining a trip to the library with their work trip also appear to use libraries farther from home than do people whose library trips involve no other stops (Table 22). For each of the two cases in which the sample is large enough for conclusions to be valid, the radius for trips involving workplace is larger than the corresponding radius for home–library–home trips.

TABLE 21

Other Stops on Library Trip

	Richmond	Columbia	Haddington	Lovett	Wadsworth	Wynnefield	Frankford
Adults (percent of respondents)							
Home	89.9	72.4	77.4	67.0	62.4	68.4	59.2
Work	5.5	11.2	5.6	4.8	2.2	4.5	9.1
Shopping	2.8	7.7	6.1	18.2	30.1	15.5	23.8
Other or no answer	1.8	8.7	10.9	10.0	5.3	11.6	7.9
Children (percent of respondents)							
Home	80.5	75.9	73.3	76.4	64.6	67.5	58.1
School	6.6	12.9	14.7	7.3	5.9	9.5	7.1
Shopping	1.6	4.5	2.3	9.5	21.7	12.8	26.7
Other or no answer	11.3	7.5	9.7	6.8	7.8	10.2	8.1
Accessibility [a]							
To elementary and secondary schools	108.9	110.3	38.4	7.7	6.1	8.9	5.5
To commercial areas	8.9	25.5	12.1	27.8	50.1	17.7	35.9

Note: Libraries are arranged in order of increasing average distance from residence of user to library.
[a] For definition of accessibility, see Table 30.

The effect on radius of persons combining school trips with library trips, however, is not clear (Table 22). In seven cases, radii for trips involving school are longer than for home–library–home trips, but in six cases they are smaller.

Table 22 gives radii, both for all surveyed users of each library and for those who stated that they usually use the given library. In almost every case, there is no significant difference in the radius for these two groups. In each of the few situations where there is a difference, the radius of regular users is smaller than that of all users—a result which would be expected.

It can also be seen in Table 22 that, quite consistently, the radius for adults is greater than that for teen-agers, which, in turn, is greater than that for children.

Means of Transportation to Libraries

The way people get to the library also may have an effect upon the distance they are willing to travel. Walking and automobile travel are the most common ways of going to the library (Table 23). In low-income, densely built areas, nearly everyone walks. Although the Columbia branch is well served by surface transit, 80 percent of its patrons come by foot. The high percentage of users walking to the Richmond and Haddington branches may be attributed to a lack of convenient transit, as well as to the low-income characteristics of their neighborhoods. In upper-income suburban areas, the percentage of users walking to the library drops off (a low of 31 percent in Wynnefield) and the percentage coming by auto increases (a high of 53 percent in Wynnefield). Transit is used by very few, usually considerably less than 10 percent. The Frankford branch is an exception in that 18 percent use transit, probably because the library is located at a major rapid transit stop.

TABLE 22

Radii Encompassing 80 Percent of Users for Single
and Multistop Library Trips
(in miles)

	Richmond	Columbia	Haddington	Lovett	Wadsworth	Wynnefield	Frankford
All Trips							
All respondents							
Under 14	0.41	0.60	0.54	0.67	0.80	1.49	1.20
14-18	0.57	0.59	0.82	0.84	1.48	over 2	1.38
Over 18	0.50	0.75	1.17	1.10	1.85	over 2	1.50
Home-Library-Home Trips							
All respondents							
Under 14	0.45	0.62	0.60	0.62	0.74	0.87	1.17
14-18	0.57	0.56	0.80	0.86	2.00	over 2	1.13
Over 18	0.39	0.68	0.87	1.02	1.70	over 2	1.21
Respondents usually using that library							
Under 14	0.45	0.62	0.60	0.62	0.74	0.87	1.17
14-18	0.57	0.56	0.62	0.86	2.00	0.63	1.13
Over 18	0.39	0.68	0.83	1.02	1.70	0.82	1.21
Trips Involving Shopping Alone or Linked with Home							
All respondents							
Under 14				0.81	0.81	over 2	1.33
14-18				0.63	1.62	over 2	1.38
Over 18				1.20	1.80	over 2	1.50
Respondents usually using that library							
Under 14				0.81	0.81	over 2	1.20
14-18				0.63	1.62	0.63	1.38
Over 18				1.20	1.80	0.82	1.50
Trips Involving School (for Children) or Work (for Adults)							
Respondents usually using that library							
Under 14	0.31	0.50	0.42	1.25		1.75	0.62
14-18	0.75	0.57	0.42	over 2	1.32	over 2	1.37
Over 18				1.50			over 2

Note: A blank cell indicates that the sample was too small to compute a statistically reliable figure.

TABLE 23

Means of Transportation to Libraries
(in percent of respondents)

	Richmond	Columbia	Haddington	Lovett	Wadsworth	Wynnefield	Frankford
Walk	87.1	80.3	64.0	39.1	46.7	30.7	53.5
Car	10.6	4.9	30.2	51.8	43.4	52.5	25.5
Public transit	1.0	7.1	0.6	3.5	5.4	8.5	17.7
No answer	1.3	7.7	5.2	5.6	4.5	8.3	3.3

TABLE 24

Library Users from Outside Philadelphia
(percentage of respondents)

	Children under 14	Persons over 14 in Secondary School	Adults
Wadsworth	10.6	2.3	24.9
Wynnefield	5.1	21.3	20.6

The Individual Branch

Library Users from Outside of Philadelphia

Both the Wadsworth and Wynnefield branches are close to the city border and have many users from the adjoining county. These users tend to come from a much greater distance, which may mean that the suburbs are not providing library service comparable to that provided by the city system. Of all the users of these two libraries, the percentage who are nonresidents is shown in Table 24.

At the Haddington Branch no children and very few teenagers come from out of town, but 8.6 percent of the adults do, which may explain the discrepancy between the distance distribution of adults and younger users (Figure 20).

NOTES

1. The data on the age of residents of each nominal service area (chapter 4) are from U.S., Department of Commerce, Bureau of the Census, *U.S. Census of the Population: 1960* (Washington, D.C.: Government Printing Office, 1960).

2. Note that in Table 12 and subsequent tables the age categories do not correspond exactly to those used elsewhere in the report. Specifically, the category "adult" includes all persons between fourteen and eighteen years of age who are not in secondary school, in addition to all persons over eighteen years of age. This definition is an attempt to reflect the difference in life style of those in secondary school and those out of school. It cannot be used, however, in the parts of the analysis where users are related to total population, which is available from the United States Census Bureau only by age group, regardless of enrollment in secondary school.

3. However, since a high percentage of children did not answer the question concerning their father's occupation, the observations concerning occupation of parents of children cannot be considered very reliable.

4. This suggests that a better question for future surveys would

be: If you are returning a book, for what purpose, if any, did you use it?

5. The question of how to weight professional services relative to circulation is not resolved. In this computation, we counted library users served and assumed each user served was an equivalent unit of output. Other weightings might give substantially different results.

6. In general, the responses concerning dissatisfaction must be considered somewhat unreliable, since both the number of persons who did not answer and the number who gave a large number of responses is quite high. If the responses do reflect reality, there is evidently a large proportion of users who have no complaints and a large proportion who have many complaints.

7. Note that if every trip both began and ended at home, the percentage "home" in Table 21 would be 100 percent. If every trip either began *or* ended at home, the percentage "home" would be 50 percent. Such trips are far more likely than intermediate trips (such as work–library–shopping). Therefore, the low percentage of home trips at Frankford, and to a lesser extent at Wadsworth, is remarkable.

6

ANALYSIS OF THE EFFECTS OF LOCATION ON LIBRARY USE

Knowledge of the distance people are willing to travel for library service is vital to the planning of an efficient library system. If libraries are too far apart, many people will not be served. If they are too close together, services may be provided which will not be used fully. If they are spaced evenly, they may not provide equal service to persons with varying incomes and abilities to travel. These and other issues must be considered in creating an optimal library plan.

In the preceding section, certain preliminary measures have been developed, which relate library use to distance. Further measures will be developed in this chapter to provide the basis for more thorough analysis.

MARKET RADIUS

Definition and Measurement

If we define the market area of a library as that area within which 80 percent of the users of the library reside, we observe from Table 25 that, for adult users, no library has a market radius of less than about ½ mile, and most libraries have a market radius of between 1⅛ and 1⅞ miles. The choice of 80 percent of the users as the criterion to define the actual market area is arbitrary; however, it does include a large majority of the users and is free of major distortion caused by a few random users from great distances.

For teen-agers (persons over fourteen in secondary school), the 80 percent radius is shorter than for adults for nearly all libraries. The difference in radius between adults and teen-agers ranges between 1/10 and ½ miles. For children under fourteen, the market area radius is smaller still. (See Table 25.)

The 80 percent market area radius appears to bear a systematic and expected relationship to a number of variables. It appears to increase with increase in occupational status of the residents of the nominal service area [1] (Figure 25); however, the relationship is not strong. For juveniles, it lacks statistical significance at the 0.5 level, and for adults it barely attains significance.[2]

TABLE 25

Radii of the Rings Containing Residences of Library Users (in miles)[a]

	Richmond	Columbia	Haddington	Lovett	Wadsworth	Wynnefield	Frankford
Children under 14							
50%	0.25	0.40	0.32	0.48	0.32	0.64	0.81
75	0.38	0.55	0.38	0.65	0.63	1.12	1.16
80	0.41	0.60	0.54	0.67	0.80	1.49	1.20
90	0.58	0.72	0.63	0.93	1.38	over 2	1.43
Persons over 14 in secondary school							
50%	0.42	0.35	0.40	0.53	0.53	0.86	0.95
75	0.53	0.53	0.63	0.82	1.31	over 2	1.28
80	0.57	0.59	0.82	0.84	1.48	over 2	1.38
90	0.80	0.72	0.98	1.92	over 2	over 2	1.68
Adults							
50%	0.26	0.42	0.67	0.68	0.63	0.85	0.88
75	0.40	0.71	1.05	1.07	1.60	over 2	1.33
80	0.50	0.75	1.17	1.10	1.85	2.60[b]	1.50
90	0.68	1.10	1.85	1.90	over 2	over 2	over 2

[a] Rings are in general diamond-shaped, since radii were defined by actual walking distance along city streets, most of which are in a rectilinear grid.
[b] Extrapolated.

The 80 percent market area radius also appears to increase with increase in circulation level (Figure 26). The meaning of this is somewhat ambiguous; however, it appears to indicate that libraries with high circulation attract residents who live relatively far away.

The 80 percent market area radius also appears to increase with increase in bookstock. (See Figure 27.) One would expect this result since the larger the number of books available—and presumably the more varied the collection—the farther people are likely to travel to consult them. The data on bookstock, however, do not give any indication of the age or quality of the books in each library. Such data are necessary for more reliable conclusions.

Finally, as can be seen in Figure 28, the relationship between the size of the 80 percent market area radius and the average distance to the nearest and next nearest libraries is relatively weak. As libraries become farther apart, their market areas would be expected to be larger, but the relationship does not appear to be strong. There is some indication that for libraries a long distance apart, adults, particularly, may consider factors other than distance in choosing a library. This "overlap" of market areas will be explored more fully later in this chapter.

Comparison of Market Area and Nominal Service Area

It is of interest to compare the observed market areas with the nominal service areas recognized by librarians and used in the analysis of chapter 4. For two of the libraries—Richmond and Columbia—the observed market area is smaller than the nominal service area. For the other four libraries studied—Lovett, Wadsworth, Wynnefield, and Frankford—the observed market area is larger than the nominal area.

KEY FOR FIGURES 25-28:

- ✶ Columbia
- ✺ Richmond
- ○ Haddington
- ✷ Frankford
- ✳ Lovett
- ■ Wadsworth
- ✜ Wynnefield

FIGURE 25

Radius of Market Area with 80% of Users vs. Percent of Employed Adults in Nominal Service Area who are Professionals, Managers, and Officials

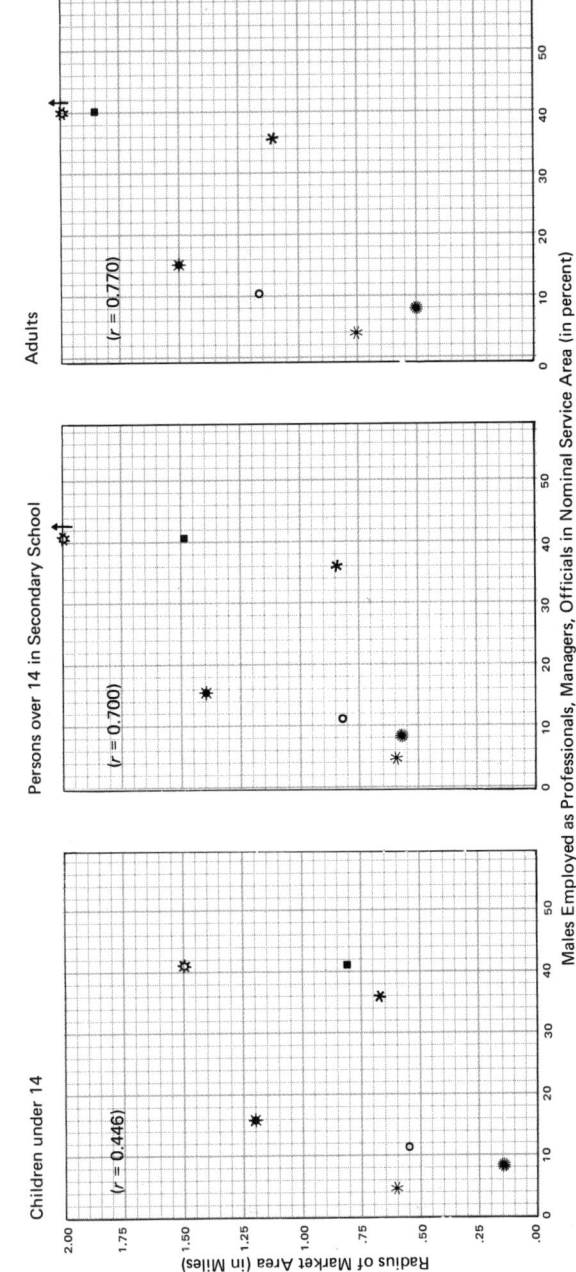

FIGURE 26

Radius of Market Area with 80% of Users vs. Annual Circulation

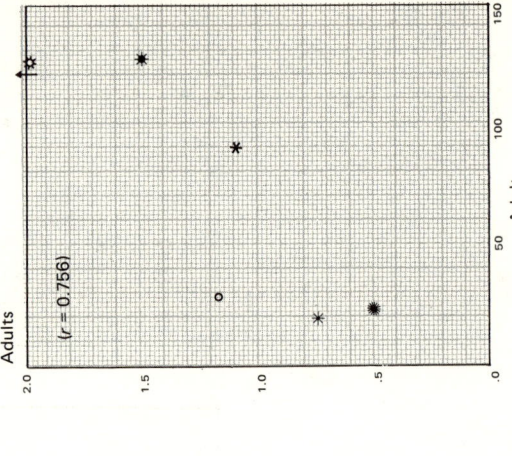

FIGURE 27

Radius of Market Area with 80% of Users vs. Bookstock

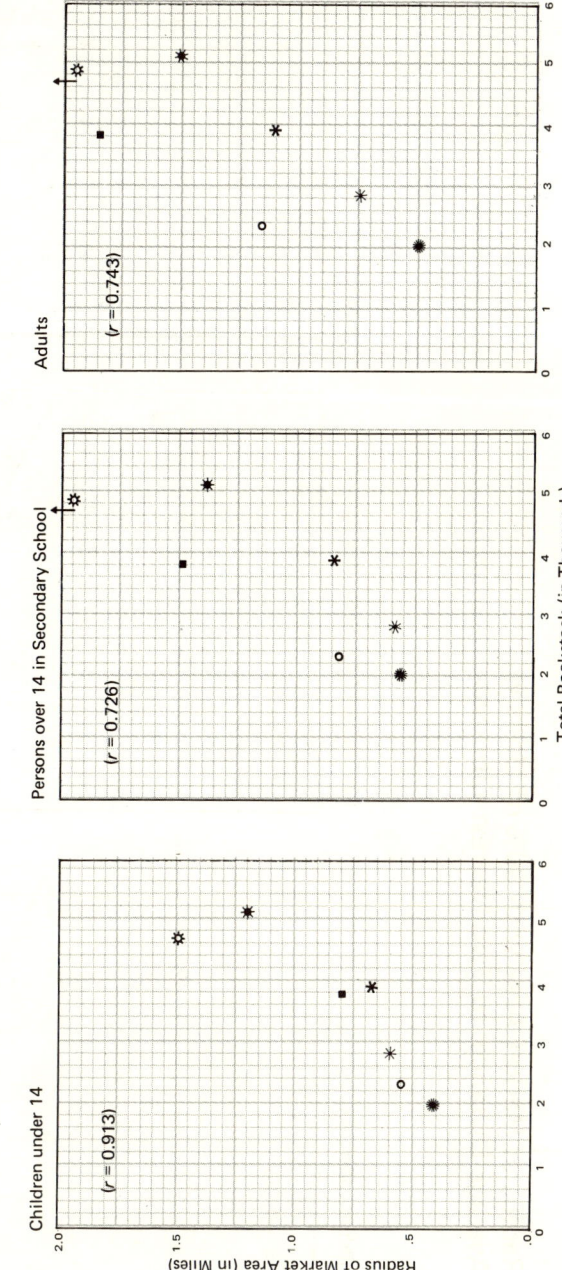

FIGURE 28

Radius of Market Area with 80% of Users vs. Average Distance to Two Nearest Libraries

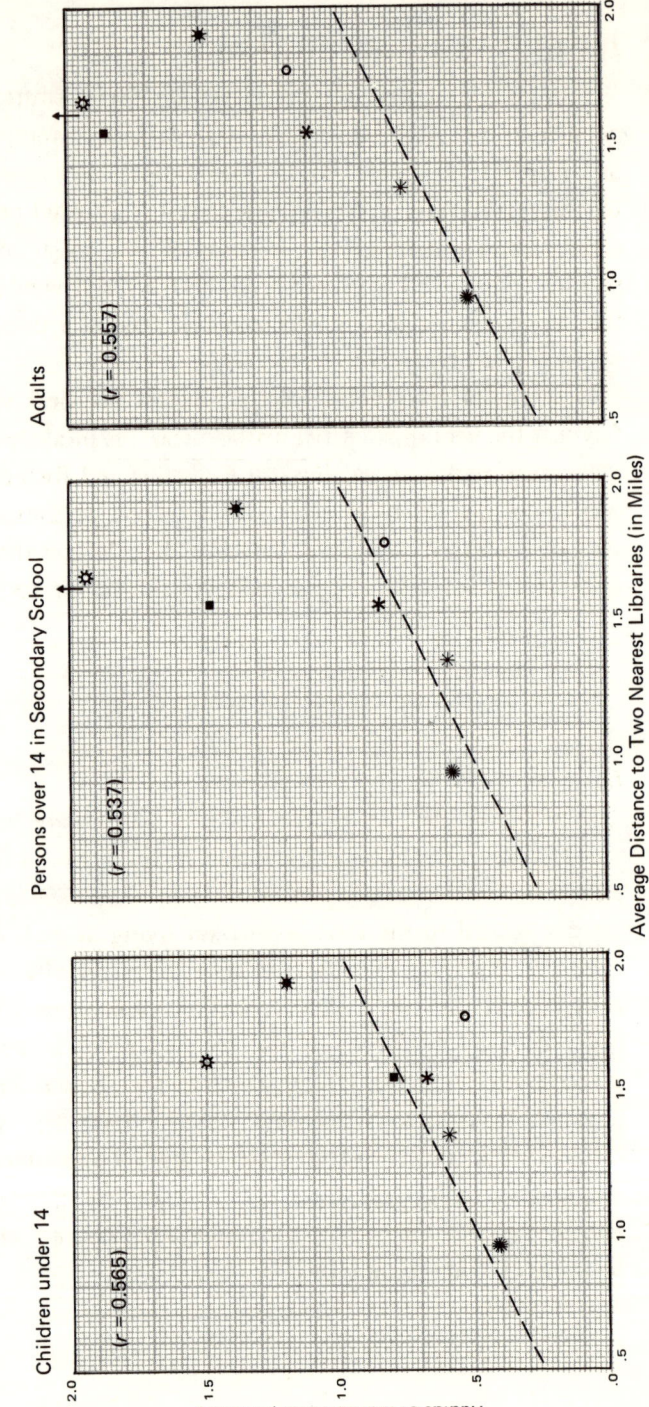

NOTE: DASHED LINE INDICATES THE PLOT WHICH WOULD RESULT IF THE 80 PERCENT RADIUS WERE EQUAL TO HALF THE AVERAGE DISTANCE TO THE NEAREST LIBRARIES.

This finding points up the rather arbitrary nature of the population base used for the per capita circulation computations in chapter 4. It appears that if the computations were to be redone on the basis of actual market areas, calculated per capita circulation would be greater in areas of low social level and smaller in areas of high social level. Such a result would reduce the importance ascribed earlier to social class as a determinant of per capita library use.

Such an interpretation, however, would not deal with the fact that the very small actual market areas (as measured by the 80 percent market area radius) of Columbia and Richmond are surrounded by extensive areas that must be presumed to be virtually unserved at present. The fact that these market areas are so small is explainable, at least in part, by the social level of the resident population.

USE RATE BY RESIDENTS

Users per 1,000 Residents by Distance
The preceding data on the residence of the library user provided a basis for defining market areas of the surveyed libraries. However, it is difficult to generalize from these data since they are not related to the total population living at each distance ring; for example, two libraries may have virtually identical market radii. But if, within its market radius, one library is being used by 1 percent of the population while within its market area the other library is attracting 10 percent of its population, obviously one would want to draw very different conclusions about the two libraries. In other words, the 80 percent market radius concept is not adequate for drawing comparison between libraries or for projecting the use that would be made of a library in a new location.

The relationship between the number of users and the number of residents at each distance is presented in Figures 29, 30, and 31 and is given in Table 26.[3] In general, this use rate drops with distance, as would be expected. The most orderly pattern seems to be that of adults, followed by that of children under fourteen.[4] The pattern for persons fourteen to eighteen years old is very irregular, though it, too, indicates a clear decline in use rate with increasing distance. The population data for this age group are particularly unreliable since the group spans only four years.

In the plot of rates of use by children (Figure 29), Frankford and Columbia stand out as libraries that do not have a high use by children at any distance. Although for both branches rates are low near the library, the Columbia rate drops off in typical fashion with increasing distance, while the Frankford rate is relatively unaffected by distance. As a result, the market radius of Frankford is unusually large. In the plot of adult use rates (Figure 31), Columbia, Haddington, and Richmond stand out as libraries that do not have a high rate of use at any distance. Rates for each of these libraries drop off gradually with distance.

The only comparable data on use rates of which we are aware come from a study of the Duluth Public Library system published in 1933. These data for branch libraries are given in Table 27. In order to make comparisons with the Philadelphia data, we have adjusted the Duluth data using the assumption that a two-day sample (such as the one made in Philadelphia) is equivalent to $2/22$ of a full month of operation of the Duluth library system. The adjusted Duluth figures, also given in Table 27, cannot be compared directly with the Philadelphia data, since the Duluth data are for all users while the Philadelphia data are given separately for age groups. However, the

KEY FOR FIGURES 29, 30, 31

━━━━━ Columbia
━━━▲━━ Richmond
··········· Haddington
─·─·─ Frankford
─ ─ ─ Lovett
▮▮▮▮▮▮▮ Wadsworth
▬ ▬ ▬ Wynnefield

NOTES: DATA HAVE BEEN ADJUSTED FOR VARYING RESPONSE RATES. THEY REFER ONLY TO PERSONS RESIDING WITHIN THE CITY OF PHILADELPHIA.

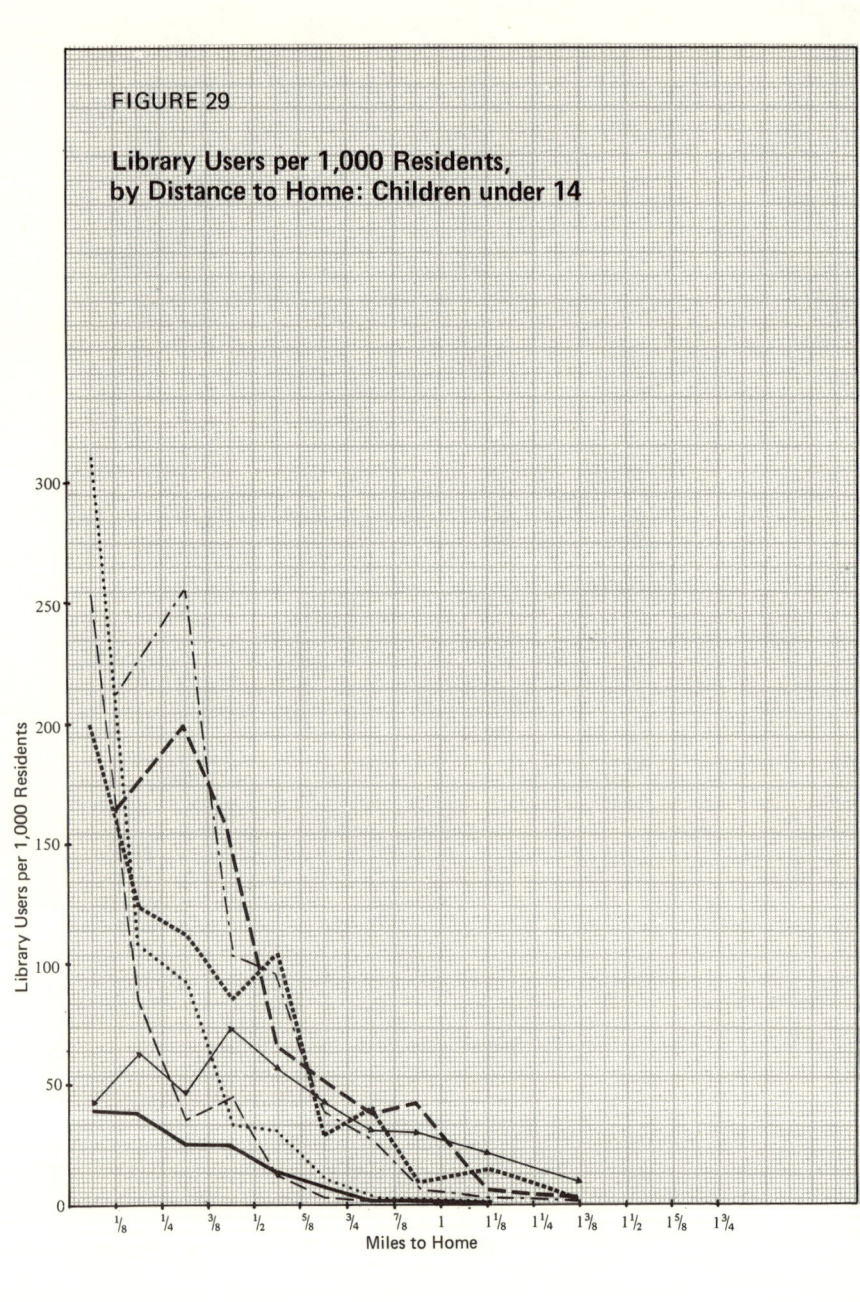

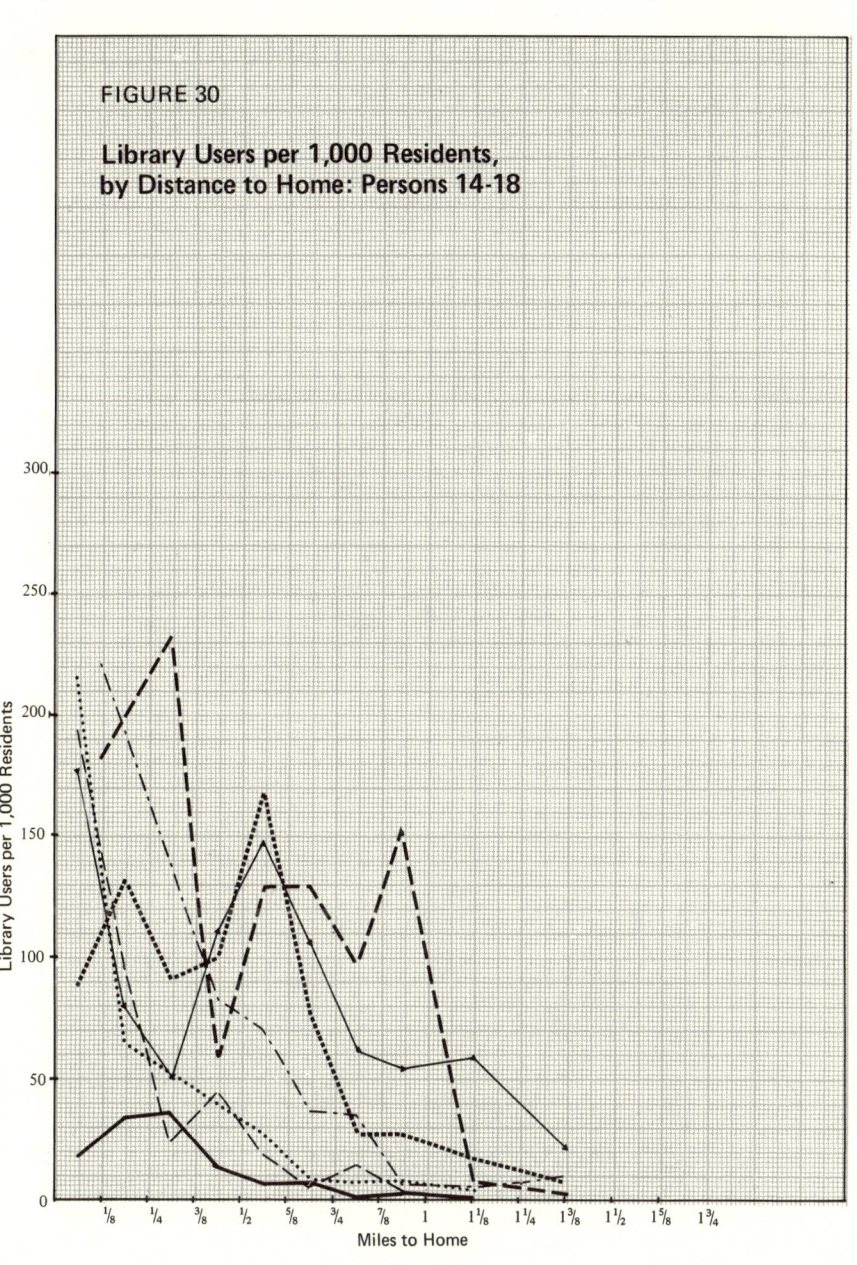

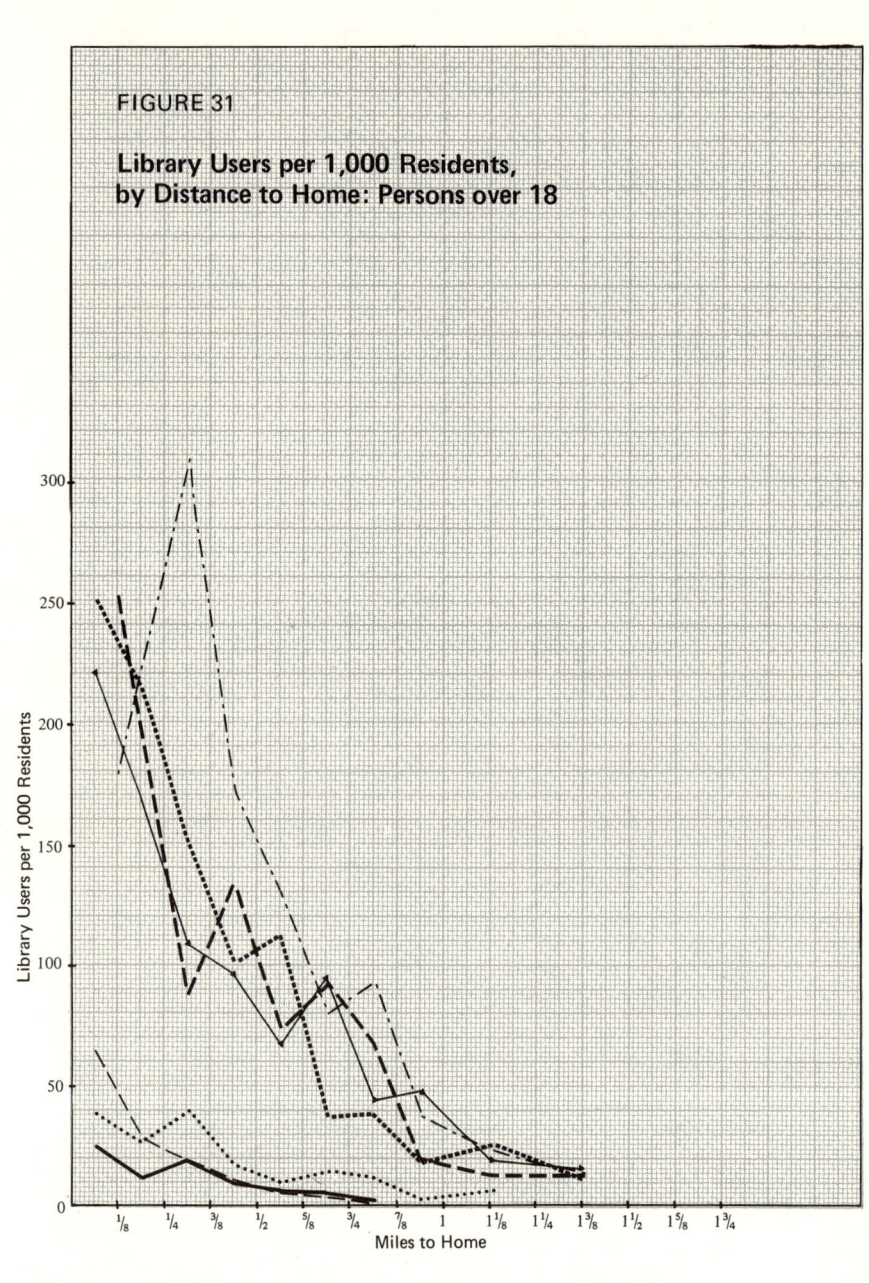

TABLE 26

Users per 1,000 Residents, by Branch, Age of User, and Distance from Home to Library

	Under 1/8 Mile	1/8–1/4 Mile	1/4–3/8 Mile	3/8–1/2 Mile	1/2–5/8 Mile	5/8–3/4 Mile	3/4–7/8 Mile	7/8–1 Mile	1–1 1/4 Mile	1 1/4–1 1/2 Mile
Columbia										
Under 14	39.6	38.4	25.8	24.9	13.5	7.2	1.9	1.7		
14–18	18.6	33.8	35.8	13.6	6.5	6.9		1.9	0.2	
Over 18	2.52	1.19	1.9	0.9	0.6	0.5	0.2			
Richmond										
Under 14	254.0	84.8	35.8	45.0	11.8	2.4	1.2	0.8	0.5	1.4
14–18	192.5	97.0	22.4	42.3	18.3	6.2	14.2	3.7	0.8	9.6
Over 18	6.50	2.82	1.94	1.02	0.42	0.28	0.17			1.4
Haddington										
Under 14	310.0	108.0	93.1	33.6	30.6	11.2	3.3	0.6	2.9	1.8
14–18	216.0	65.0	52.5	30.8	28.0	8.7	6.7	7.7	0.6	7.2
Over 18	3.98	2.6	4.0	1.7	1.0	1.4	1.1	0.3		1.1
Frankford										
Under 14	42.5	63.2	46.5	73.3	56.8	43.2	30.8	30.2	21.6	9.5
14–18	177.0	80.0	51.7	111.0	148.0	106.0	61.8	55.0	59.3	21.6
Over 18	22.2	16.9	10.9	9.6	6.7	9.5	4.4	4.8	2.9	1.5
Lovett										
Under 14	213.0[a]	213.0[a]	254.0	104.0	96.0	38.6	27.2	6.5	3.0	1.4
14–18	222.0[a]	222.0[a]	137.0	83.2	70.3	36.2	35.0	7.6	4.9	9.6
Over 18	18.0[a]	18.0[a]	30.9	17.3	13.1	8.0	9.3	3.8	2.4	1.4
Wadsworth										
Under 14	198.0	124.0	112.5	86.0	105.2	28.7	39.6	8.9	15.0	1.8
14–18	88.7	131.0	90.4	98.8	166.0	77.7	26.8	26.7	16.7	7.2
Over 18	25.1	21.4	15.1	10.1	11.3	3.7	3.8	1.8	2.6	1.1
Wynnefield										
Under 14	164.0[a]	164.0[a]	199.0	153.5	66.0	51.0	87.6	42.2	4.7	2.5
14–18	182.0[a]	182.0[a]	232.0	58.5	129.5	129.0	97.5	152.0	7.4	2.2
Over 18	25.3[a]	25.3[a]	8.9	13.4	7.3	9.3	6.8	1.9	1.2	1.3

Note: Data have been adjusted for varying response rates. They refer only to persons residing within the city of Philadelphia. See Chapter 6 for method of estimating population in each distance ring. Blank cells indicate less than 0.1.

[a] Computed over 0–1/4 mile range as a whole.

use rates in Duluth in 1933 appear to be generally lower than those in Philadelphia in 1966 and appear to drop off with distance at a slower rate.

Definition of Use Rate Concepts

The data on use rates in this chapter suggest that there are some basic properties of library use rates that would be helpful in comparing libraries and planning library systems. These properties are the highest rate of use (usually of residents in the vicinity of the library) and the decline in use rate with distance from the library. These two properties together should establish a service area for each library that can be related to the characteristics of resident population, of users, and of the library itself.

The use rate in the immediate vicinity of the library out to a radius of ¼ miles is defined as the base level use rate. (See Table 28.) It is assumed that the use rates of residents in this immediate neighborhood are not significantly affected by distance to the library. The base level use rate of any particular library is, therefore, hypothesized to depend only upon the desire of neighboring residents for the library service and upon the quality of the library itself.

There are two ways of viewing the decline in use rate with increasing distance from the library. One is to measure the distance at which use rate first drops to some nominal level. This "effective service radius" is defined as the distance from the library at which use rate is 10 percent of the base level use rate.[5] This measure is different from the 80 percent market area radius, which is given for comparison in Table 28.

A second approach is to measure the rate of decline in use with distance. The absolute decline per mile is measured over the effective service radius. It is equal to 90 percent of the base

The Effects of Location on Library Use

level use rate divided by the effective service radius. The relative decline per mile is the absolute decline as a percentage of the base level use rate. These measures for the seven libraries and the detailed method of computation are given in Table 28.

Statistical Explanation of Effective Service Radius and Base Level Use Rate

The effective service radius and the base level use rate measure different properties of the pattern of use of any given library. That these properties are distinct can be inferred from Figure 32. The plot indicates that there is probably only a weak relationship between the two properties ($r = -0.305$ for juveniles and 0.646 for adults). To be significant at the 0.05 level, a minimum value of 0.7067 is necessary. Therefore, in order to estimate the pattern of use of a library, it is necessary to estimate each of the two properties separately.

The results reported in chapter 4 indicate that the use made of a library is determined primarily by the size and quality of the library and by the general social environment in which the library is located. The best available measure of size and quality of a library was found, in that chapter, to be bookstock. The best available measure of social environment was found to be the percentage of employed adults who are managers, professionals, or officials. For the seven libraries in the survey, data on bookstock and occupational level are given in Table 29.

BASE LEVEL USE RATE Base level use rate for adults is explained to a large extent by the occupational level of the residents in the nominal service area of the library. (See Figure 34, where $r = 0.933$ for adults.) For juveniles, the correlation just fails to be statistically significant ($r = 0.618$). As can be seen in Figure 33, the total bookstock in the library appears to have no effect on the base level use rate of juveniles ($r = 0.040$), but

TABLE 27

Number of Book Borrowers by Distance of Residence,
Duluth Public Library System, 1933

Miles from Residence to Library	Borrowers per Month			
	2 Branches in Main Portion of City		3 Branches in Isolated Suburbs	
	Per 1,000 Residents	Index	Per 1,000 Residents	Index
0–1/4	470	100	840	100
1/4–1/2	280	60	560	67
1/2–3/4	200	43	400	48
3/4–1	90	19	190	23

Miles from Residence to Library	Number of Borrowers in Two-Day Sample Period (estimate)			
	Per 1,000 Residents	Index	Per 1,000 Residents	Index
0–1/4	43	100	76	100
1/4–1/2	25	60	51	67
1/2–3/4	18	43	36	48
3/4–1	8	19	17	23

Source: Estimated from charts presented by A. B. Horwitz, "Effect of Distance upon Frequency of Use of Public Library Facilities," *City Planning* 9, no. 3 (July 1933): 135-137.

TABLE 28

Base Level Use Rate, Effective Service Radius, Market Area
Radius, and Decline in Use Rate per Mile

	Base Level Use Rate[a] (users per 1,000 residents)		Radius of Effective Service Area[b] (in miles)		Market Area Radius[c] (in miles)		Decline in Adult Use Rate per Mile[d]	
	Under 14 years	Adults	Under 14 years	Adults	Under 14 years	Adults	Absolute	Relative to base level
Columbia	40.6	1.54	0.75	0.77	0.60	0.75	1.80	1.17
Richmond	131.0	3.78	0.56	0.67	0.41	0.50	5.08	1.35
Haddington	165.0	3.57	0.66	0.92	0.54	1.17	3.49	0.98
Frankford	59.6	17.90	1.45	1.18	1.20	1.50	13.60	0.76
Lovett	212.0	24.24	0.85	1.12	0.67	1.10	19.50	0.80
Wadsworth	146.0	22.40	0.92	0.93	0.80	1.85	21.70	0.97
Wynnefield	159.0	28.30	1.07	0.94	1.49	2.60	27.10	0.92

[a]Within 1/4 mile of library. Number of users is number of users during the survey (one weekday with evening hours and one Saturday).
[b]Radius to point where use rate is 1/10 that at base level.
[c]Radius of area including 80 percent of all users. See chapter 6. The age group "adults" includes persons over fourteen years not in school, as well as all persons over eighteen years. See chapter 5. Radius for Wynnefield adult users was estimated by extrapolation.
[d]Decline in adult users per 1,000 residents. Decline is measured over effective service radius. Since use rate, by definition, declines by 90 percent over this radius, the decline per mile is 0.90 x base level use rate divided by effective service radius.

TABLE 29

Bookstock of Library and Occupational Level of
Residents of Service Area and of Users

	Professionals in Nominal Service Area[a] (in percent)	Total Professional Users[b] (in percent)	Bookstock[c]
Columbia	4.9	23.5	28,316
Richmond	8.6	6.1	20,063
Haddington	11.6	48.0	23,900
Frankford	16.0	33.7	51,412
Lovett	36.4	69.4	39,463
Wadsworth	41.2	60.9	38,447
Wynnefield	41.4	64.9	47,693

[a]Nominal service areas are defined by librarians and used in chapter 4. "Professionals" refers to males employed as professionals, managers, or officials. U.S. Census of Population: 1960.
[b]From survey.
[c]Provided by the Free Library of Philadelphia.

The Effects of Location on Library Use 119

has a significant effect for adults ($r = 0.833$). In addition, it does not appear that bookstock would explain the deviations from the base level rates that would be predicted by social level. The data, however, are very limited. All libraries but Frankford show a strong positive relationship between bookstock and the percentage of residents who are professional. We lack examples of libraries with large bookstock in areas of low social status or of libraries with small bookstock in areas of high social status.

It is apparent that very great differences in use rates occur among libraries. The base level use rates at Columbia, Richmond and Haddington are only one-tenth the level of the base level use rates at Lovett, Wadsworth, or Wynnefield; that is, the highest rates of use at the first three libraries are comparable to the use rates found at the radius of effective service of the latter three libraries.

EFFECTIVE SERVICE RADIUS The percentage of professionals, managers, and officials in the nominal service area of a library appears to bear little relationship to the effective service radius of the library (Figure 36). A very strong relationship, however, exists between size of bookstock and effective service radius, particularly for juveniles (Figure 35).

Unlike the base level use rate, the radius of the effective service area discussed above varies over a rather limited range, the largest radius for adults being about 1.75 times as large as the smallest.[6]

DECLINE IN USE RATE PER MILE The absolute decline in the adult use rate ranges between 1.80 users per mile for Columbia to 27.70 users per mile for Wadsworth (Table 28). Absolute decline corresponds closely to base level use rate, as would be expected, since use rate typically drops to a tenth of the base level use rate within about one mile.

The large absolute declines in use rate per mile for libraries

KEY FOR FIGURES 32-38:

- ✳ Columbia
- ✸ Richmond
- ο Haddington
- ✱ Frankford
- ∗ Lovett
- ■ Wadsworth
- ☼ Wynnefield

FIGURE 32 **Effective Service Radius vs. Base Level Use Rate**

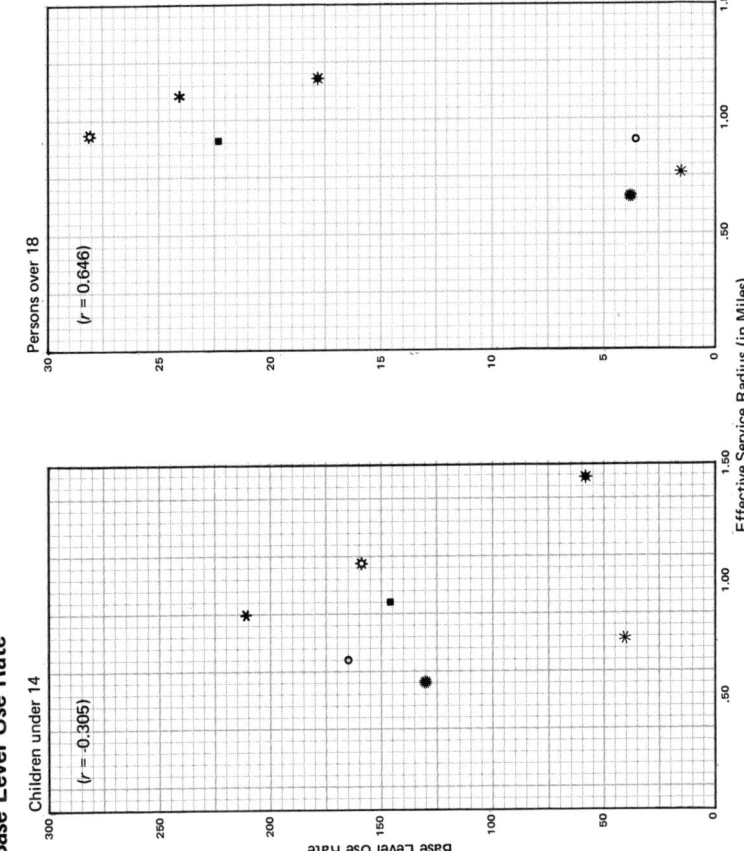

FIGURE 33

Base Level Use Rate vs. Bookstock

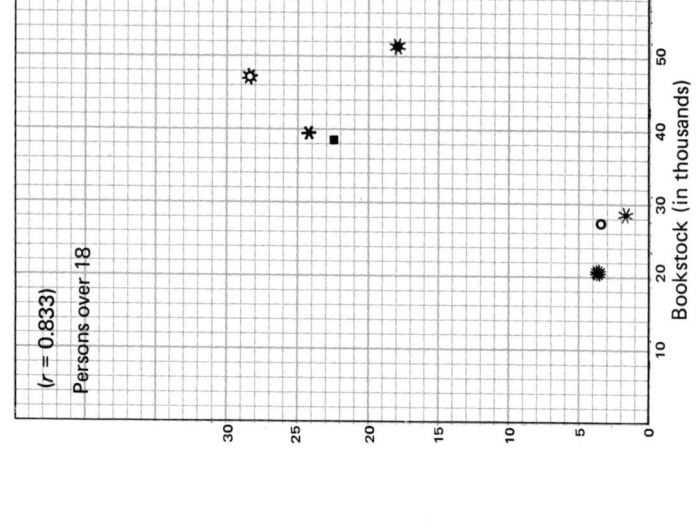

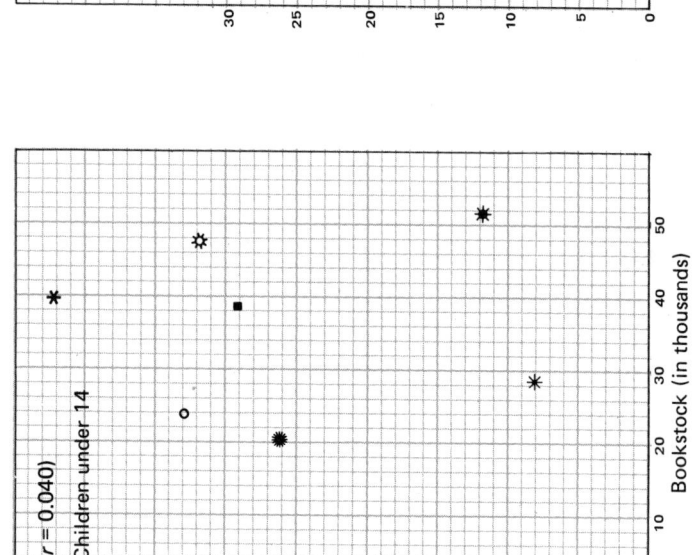

FIGURE 34

Base Level Use Rate vs. Percent Professionals, Managers, Officials in Service Area

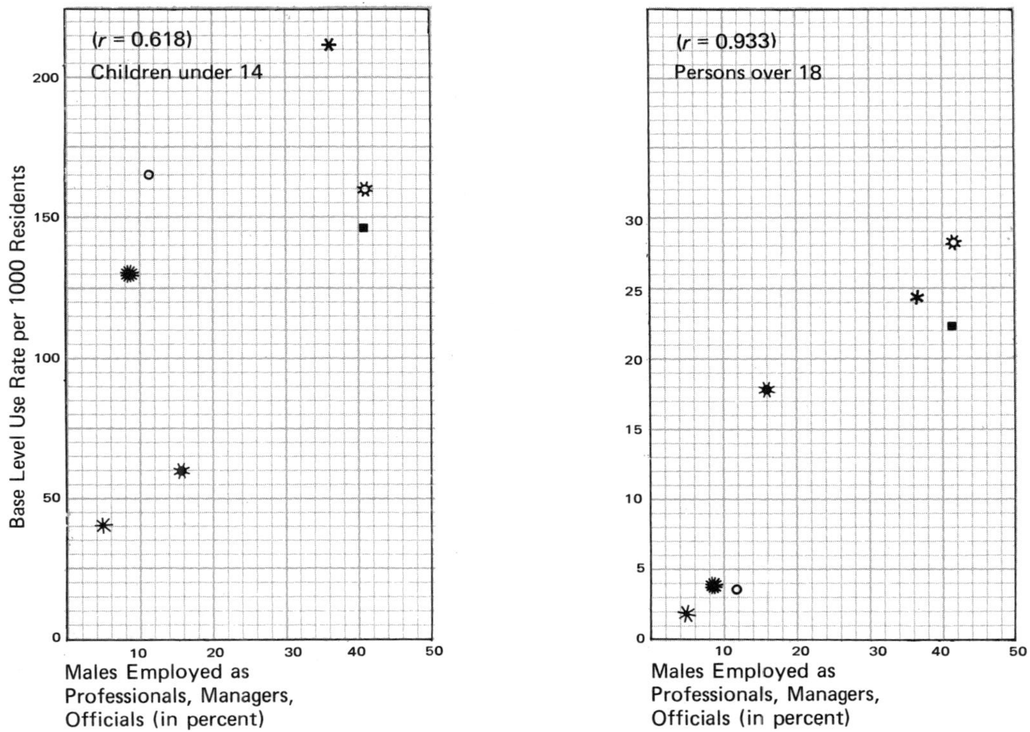

FIGURE 35   Effective Service Radius vs. Bookstock

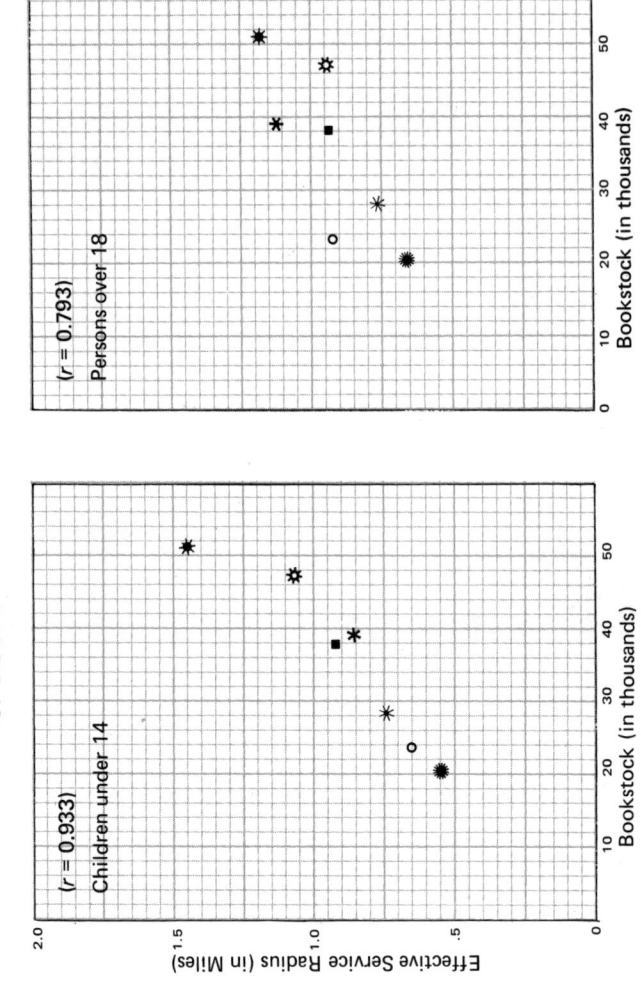

FIGURE 36 **Effective Service Radius vs. Percent Professionals, Managers, Officials in Service Area**

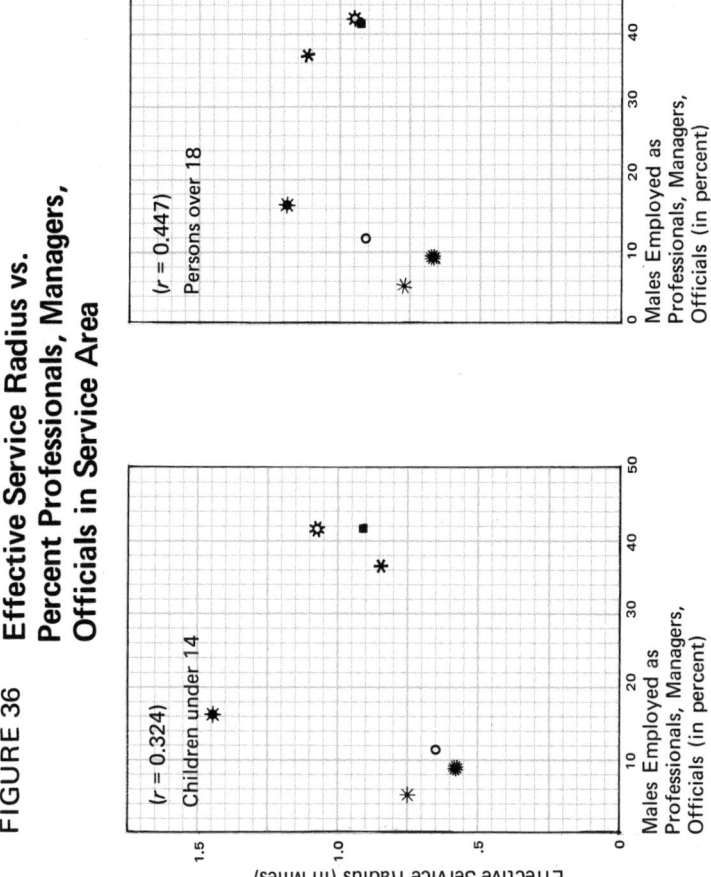

FIGURE 37 Radius of Effective Service Area vs. 80% Market Area Radius

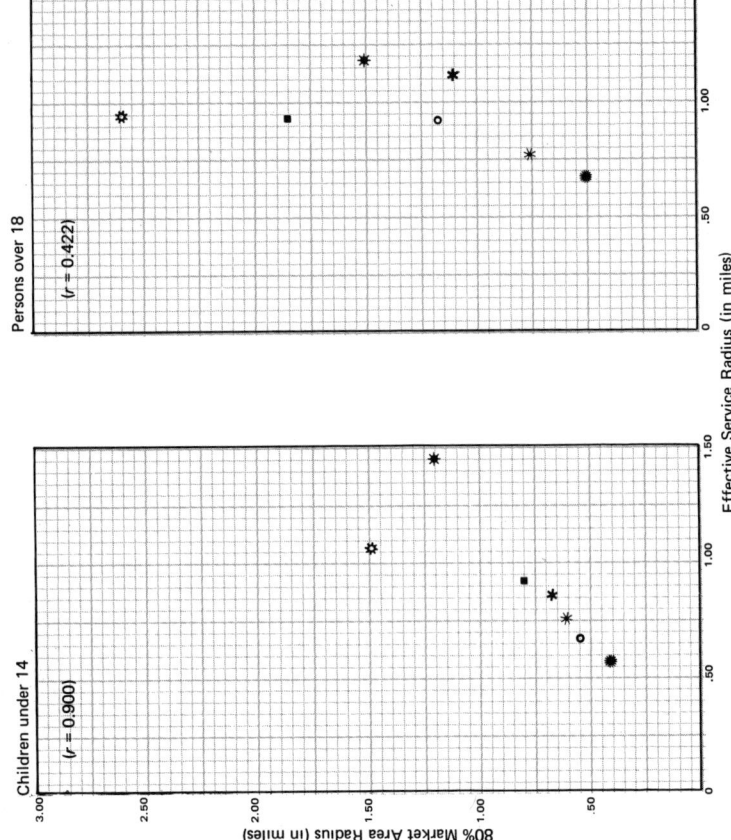

FIGURE 38

Percent of Adult Users Who Make Shopping Stop on Library Trip vs. Commercial Index

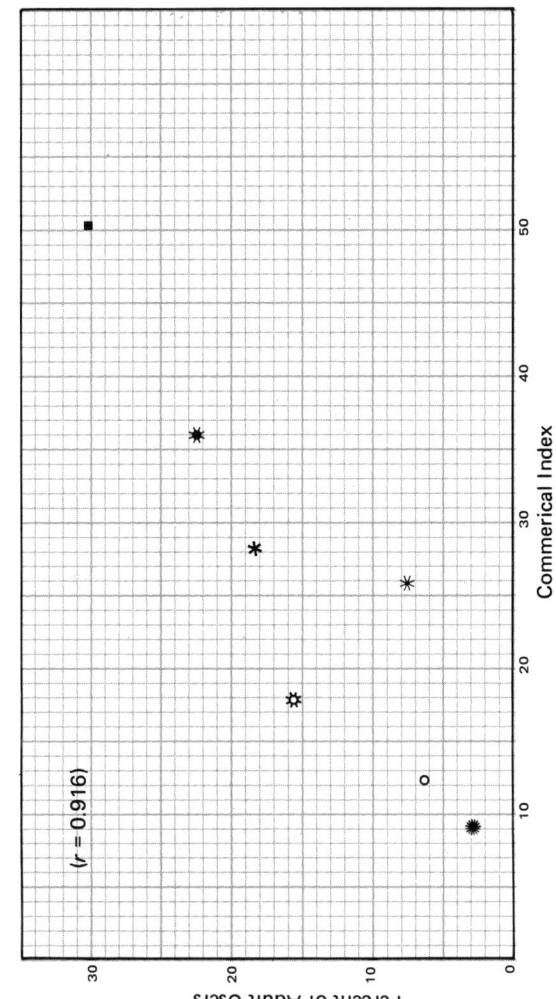

with service areas of high socioeconomic status and the low absolute declines for areas of low status are not apparent when relative decline is examined. Except for the two libraries in the neighborhood of lowest socioeconomic status, the percent decline in use rate per mile is fairly constant. If there is any systematic tendency, it is for the percent decline to fall with rising socioeconomic level of neighborhoods.

Even for low-income areas, the percent decline is only moderately greater than that for high-income areas. The percent decline for Richmond, which is the highest at 135 percent per mile, is slightly less than two standard deviations from the mean of 99 percent. Columbia's decline is less than one standard deviation above the mean. The lowest percentage is for Frankford, which is a middle-income area, rather than for Wynnefield or Wadsworth, which are high-income areas. This finding conflicts with the normal expectation that users from high-income areas would be much less sensitive to distance than users from low-income areas, who generally are presumed to be less mobile.

One possible explanation for the greater decline in high-income areas is that high-income users have alternatives to library use. They may, for example, substitute purchased books for library books to reduce the inconvenience of long trips to the library. The low rate of decline over the middle-income service area for the Frankford branch may be explained by its location near a major rapid transit stop, which extends the effective service radius. This may suggest the importance of easy and inexpensive transportation in reducing the rate of decline of use with distance. It is likely that transit availability does not increase use by residents in the near vicinity as much as it increases use by more distant residents.

Thus, while an additional unit of distance deters a larger absolute number of people of high socioeconomic status from using the library, the effect of distance on use relative to demand is about the same for the two groups, or, if anything, discourages low-income users more.

EFFECTIVE SERVICE RADIUS AND MARKET AREA RADIUS It is interesting to compare the effective service radius with the 80 percent market area radius, which was presented earlier in this chapter and which is given again in Table 28. The correlation between these two measures is shown in Figure 37.

For persons under fourteen years old, the two radii are almost identical for all libraries but Wynnefield ($r = 0.900$). For persons over eighteen, however, the 80 percent market radius has a low correlation ($r = 0.422$) with the effective service radius. This can probably be explained by the fact that for the Wynnefield and Wadsworth libraries particularly, a large proportion of the users come from out of town (see Table 24) and, therefore, from greater distances. The use rate computation is based only on Philadelphia users, while the 80 percent market radius computation includes the out-of-town users. Therefore, Wynnefield and Wadsworth, especially, fall outside the general pattern for adults in Figure 37.

IMPLICATIONS FOR LIBRARY SYSTEM PLANNING The correlations between base level use rate and occupational level and between bookstock and effective service radius suggest some limited conclusions for library system planning policy. If the base level use rate depends mainly on occupational and educational status and is relatively independent of bookstock, our analysis suggests that base level use rates may be raised only by major efforts of society, such as increasing educational levels and economic opportunities. These programs are beyond the jurisdiction of the library planner. At the same time, the effective service radius, which is correlated with bookstock, is probably not strongly influenced by bookstock. On the contrary, the size of the bookstock appears to be related to, and probably determined by, the demand for books.[7] Thus, libraries that experience heavy use are likely to demand and receive increasing budgets for books.

The heaviness of use is a function of both the base level use rate and the effective service radius. However, the strong correlation is with the latter, rather than with the former. If, in fact, there is a causal relationship between size of bookstock and effective service radius, it would be possible to extend market coverage of a library by expanding bookstock. This would mean that the percent decline in use rate per mile would be reduced and greater use would be encouraged by residents farther from the library. Such a policy would be an alternative to the placing of libraries closer together in order to increase total use. Either policy might lead to an overlap of service areas. Such an overlap, although it might appear inefficient, would also increase the choice of branches to visit. Given the diversity of work, shopping, and school trip patterns, this would increase the effective accessibility of the library system and should increase total use.

The question of market overlap and the effect of accessibility to schools and commercial areas are discussed later in the chapter. Other implications of these results for library system planning are discussed in chapter 7.

Effect of Accessibility on Basic System Variables to Schools and Commercial Areas

It has been hypothesized, as noted in chapter 4, that branch libraries located near schools will attract more use by juveniles than would otherwise be expected. Similarly, libraries located near or in commercial areas are expected to attract more than average use by adults. In order to explore these hypotheses,

The Effects of Location on Library Use

measurements of the accessibility of public and parochial schools and of commercial areas were made for each library. (See Table 30.) The accessibility measures take the form of the size of each school or commercial area divided by the square of the distance to it.[8] The size of a school is given by the number of pupils enrolled, and the size of a commercial area is given by the acreage in commercial land use. Distance in miles was measured from the library along streets. The exact distance was measured to each school, but for commercial areas distance "rings" were drawn around each library, and all commercial land within each ring was considered to be at the average distance of that ring.

EXPLANATION OF BASIC SYSTEM VARIABLES Contrary to our hypothesis, high accessibility to schools is associated with a low base level use rate, a short effective service radius, and a short market radius (Table 31). These correlations are significant (at the 5 percent level) for adult users, but not for juvenile users. In all cases the correlation is negative. Since we expected school accessibility to affect juvenile use, we can only conclude that the effect is not noticeable in our small sample.

There may be no causal connection, however, between accessibility to schools and the various measures of use rate and radius. Accessibility to schools is also negatively, and significantly, associated with all measures of social and economic status and with bookstock. These variables are so powerful that they outweigh any positive effects which location near a school might have. Thus, nearness of a school to a library with small bookstock in a poor neighborhood will not have enough influence to raise use rates to levels comparable to those of a library with a larger bookstock in a better neighborhood. Accessibility to schools is correlated positively and significantly with measures of user comfort (floor space per user and floor space divided by

TABLE 30

Accessibility of Libraries to Schools and to
Commercial Areas

	Elementary and Secondary Schools[a]	Commercial Areas[b]
Columbia	110.3	25.5
Richmond	108.9	8.9
Haddington	38.4	12.1
Frankford	5.5	35.9
Lovett	7.7	27.8
Wadsworth	6.1	50.1
Wynnefield	8.9	17.4

Sources: Number of pupils in public and parochial schools from The Bulletin Almanac and Yearbook for 1965 (Philadelphia: The Bulletin Company, 1965).

Land area of commercial uses and all distances from the Philadelphia City Planning Commission's 1965 land use map.

[a] Accessibility to schools within 0.5 miles $= \sum \dfrac{\text{no. pupils in school}}{(\text{distance from library to school})^2}$

[b] Accessibility to commercial areas within 0.2 miles $= \sum \dfrac{\text{area in commercial land use in ring}}{(\text{average distance from library to ring})^2}$

The distance rings were defined: 0 mi. < d_1 < 0.05 mi.; .05 mi. < d_2 < 0.10 mi.; and 0.10 mi. < d_3 < 0.20 mi. Respective average distances are 0.025, 0.075, and 0.15 miles.

TABLE 31

Correlations of Accessibility to Schools and Accessibility
to Commercial Areas with Basic System Variables and
Measures of Library Comfort

Basic System variables	Accessibility to Elementary and Secondary Schools	Accessibility to Commercial Areas
Base level use rate		
Under 14	−0.452	−0.167
Over 18	−0.845	0.479
Effective service radius		
Under 14	−0.660	0.530
Over 18	−0.852	0.480
80% market radius		
Under 14	−0.633	0.284
Adults	−0.746	0.322
Comfort level variables		
Floor space per user	0.830	−0.886
Comfort index[a]	0.851	−0.774

Source: For data sources, see Tables 19, 28, and 31.

Note: Minimum coefficient for significance at 5 percent level is 0.7067.

[a] Floor space / users x bookstock

users times bookstock). Thus, the fact that libraries highly accessible to schools do not attain high use rates cannot be attributed to crowded conditions.

Accessibility to commercial areas is positively associated with all but one of the basic system variables, but it is not significantly correlated with any of them (Table 31). It is negatively correlated with the two comfort level variables: the greater the accessibility to commercial areas, the more crowded the library.

EXPLANATION OF RESIDUALS FROM EXPECTED VALUES OF BASIC SYSTEM VARIABLES   If the accessibility measures do not provide a convincing explanation of the basic system variables themselves, it is probably because of the overpowering effect on them of variations in the socioeconomic level and the size of bookstock. If this is true, the accessibility measures might still be expected to provide a significant explanation of the variation which remains after regression with the social and bookstock variables.

The residuals from the expected effective service radius based on bookstock were correlated with the accessibility measures. Residuals from the regression with bookstock were chosen, since, as was shown earlier (Figure 35), effective service radius was explained quite well by bookstock. For juvenile users, the residuals are explained largely by accessibility to schools ($r = 0.809$). For adult users, however, little additional explanation is achieved by accessibility to commercial areas ($r = 0.090$).

Base level use rate for adults was seen earlier to be strongly correlated with percent professionals in the nominal service area ($r = 0.933$); the correlation for juveniles was less strong. (See Figure 34.) The residuals from the regressions of base level use rate on percent professionals are not well explained by the measures of accessibility. (See Table 32.) A plot of accessibility to schools against residual base level use rate of juveniles indicated such a weak relationship that the correlation coefficient was not computed. Accessibility of commercial areas yielded a correlation coefficient of only 0.120 with the residual base level use rate of adults.

In summary, the investigations of the residuals indicate that accessibility to schools may have an important influence on effective service radius for juveniles, and, therefore, it may be sensible public policy to locate libraries near schools. The apparent lack of relationship (Table 32) between accessibility to commercial areas and either base level use rate or effective service radius for adults casts some doubt upon the now generally accepted planning principle that libraries and other public facilities should be grouped in accessible community and commercial centers.[9]

This principle should not be abandoned, however, just because no strong association is apparent between library use levels and accessibility levels. It is evident from our data that there is a strong positive correlation between the commercial index and the percentage of adult users who make a shopping stop on a

TABLE 32

Correlations between Accessibility and Residuals from Regressions with Bookstock and Percent Professionals in Nominal Service Area

Residual of:	Accessibility to Schools	Accessibility to Commercial Areas
Effective service radius for under 14		
from regression with % professionals		
from regression with bookstock	0.809	
Effective service radius for over 18		
from regression with % professionals		0.301
from regression with bookstock		0.090
Base level use rate for under 14		
from regression with % professionals	low	
from regression with bookstock		
Base level use rate for over 18		
from regression with % professionals		0.120
from regression with bookstock		

Note: A blank cell indicates that the correlation was not computed.

library trip. (Figure 38) Nearly 24 percent of the Frankford adult patrons and 30 percent of the Wynnefield adult patrons make a stop for shopping on their library trip. Even if accessibility to a commercial area does not in fact increase library use, it does increase trip efficiency in general by making it possible to combine a shopping trip with a library trip in place of two separate trips. As long as location close to commercial areas does not result in fewer library trips than otherwise expected, the increase in overall urban efficiency must be counted as a net gain.

Note on Estimation of 1966 Population by Census Block

The 1966 population data on which the library use rates are computed are estimates based on detailed census data for 1960 and on trends in birth, death, and migration rates between 1960 and 1966. Death rates were applied to the population of each tract to obtain hypothetical "aged" population for 1966. This aged population was then adjusted for migration by applying a ratio derived from City Planning Commission population estimates for 1964.[10] The composite ratio containing effects of aging and migration was obtained for each census tract and was applied in turn to the estimated 1960 population of each block in the tract to yield estimated population in 1966.

This computation requires the assumptions that for all blocks in a census tract, average household size was uniform in 1960, birth and death rates between 1960 and 1966 were uniform, and gross population changes between 1960 and 1964, as estimated by the City Planning Commission, were uniform. Therefore, although it is hoped that the population estimates give a better representation of 1966 population than the 1960 census does, it is clear that considerable error may have been introduced by the assumptions required. The curves, effective radii, and other results of this section must be interpreted with this possible error in mind.

OVERLAP OF MARKET AREAS

The survey data indicate that at most libraries there are some users who visit more than one library or who use a library farther from their residence than the nearest one. This means that the basic system variables will be affected to some extent by such multiple use or use outside one's neighborhood. If large numbers of persons pass by the nearest branch library to use another one, then we can conclude that users perceive important differences between branches. However, if persons tend to use the nearest library, we can conclude that all branches are viewed as standard or equivalent. If persons do in fact differentiate between branch libraries, this could have important effects on the conclusions of the study and the implications of the study for system planning.

Definition of Penetration and Overlap

Penetration of the market area of library A by library B is defined as occurring when residents of an area use library B even though the area is closer to library A. Penetration is complete when the residents use the most distant library exclusively.

Interpenetration (overlap) of market areas occurs when, in a given residential area, some persons use library A and some persons use library B. Under these definitions, overlap cannot occur without penetration. However, penetration can occur without overlap. These concepts are diagramed in Figure 39.

Of the seven libraries surveyed, two pairs—Wadsworth and Lovett and Wynnefield and Haddington—are close enough so that considerable interpenetration occurs.

FIGURE 39

The Concepts of Penetration and Overlap

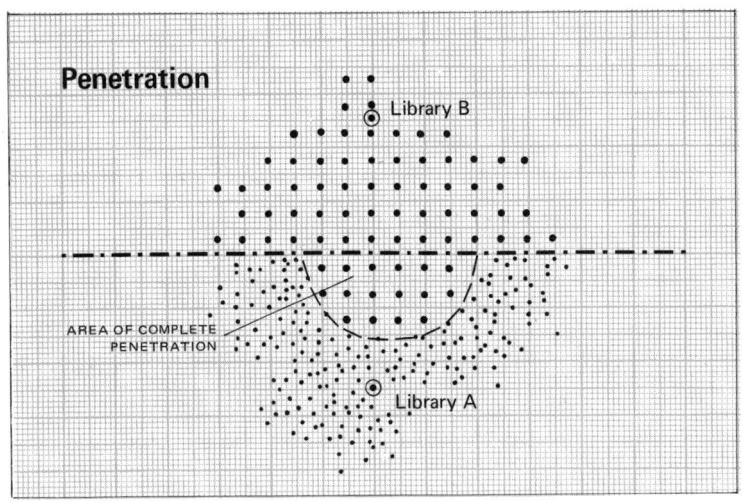

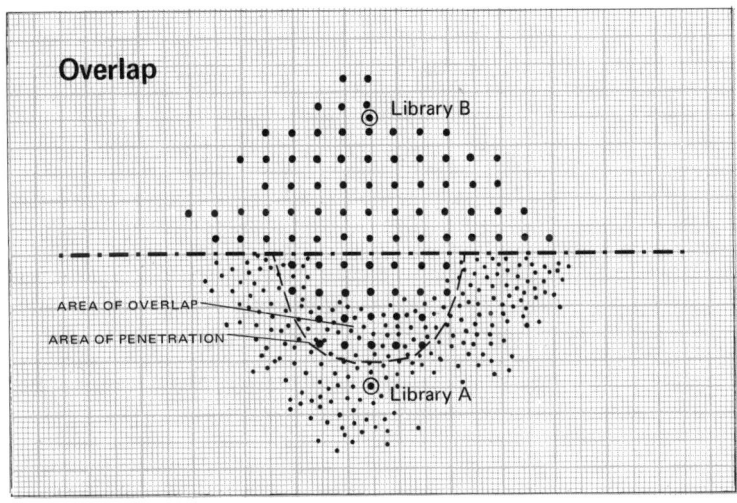

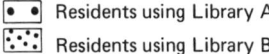 Residents using Library A
Residents using Library B

138 Urban Analysis for Branch Library System Planning

*Penetration by Two Neighboring Libraries into
Each Other's Market Area*

The Wadsworth and Lovett branches are $1^{11}/_{16}$ miles apart. Their market areas can be analyzed from the data in Table 33. In this table, the number of users is given in parentheses; the other numbers refer to the users of Lovett Library. The distance of the user's home from Wadsworth Library is given on the horizontal axis; the distance from Lovett Library is shown on the vertical axis. Therefore, entries in cells above the diagonal represent library users who lived closer to Lovett Library. If no penetration had occurred, all such persons would have used Lovett Library. The number of users above the diagonal who used Wadsworth (in parentheses) is a measure of the penetration of Lovett's market area by Wadsworth. Similarly, the numbers without parentheses below the diagonal represent the number of people who used Lovett even though they lived closer to Wadsworth.

Wadsworth attracted a few more users from Lovett's natural market area than did Lovett from Wadsworth's. Twenty-two adults [11] used Wadsworth although they lived closer to Lovett, while nineteen adults used Lovett although they lived closer to Wadsworth. For children, the pattern is similar, but the contrast is more extreme. Seven children used Wadsworth although they lived closer to Lovett; only one used Lovett although he lived closer to Wadsworth. In total, 4.0 percent of all persons using Wadsworth lived closer to Lovett, and 2.6 percent of all persons using Lovett lived closer to Wadsworth. These percentages, which are small, relate to the penetration into the market area of only one neighboring library. Penetration into all neighboring market areas is 15.2 percent for Wadsworth and 9.8 percent for Lovett (see final section of this chapter).

TABLE 33

Penetration and Overlap of Lovett and Wadsworth Market Areas

Adults

Miles from Residence to Lovett	\\	1/2-3/4	3/4-1	Miles from Residence to Wadsworth 1-1 1/4	1 1/4-1 1/2	1 1/2-1 3/4	1 3/4-2
1/2-3/4	—	—	(0) 6	(2) 13	(0) 17	(0) 8	(2) 10
3/4-1	(1) 1	\\	(10) 9	(8) 16	(3) 11	(0) 5	(0) 3
1-1 1/4	(14) 3	(4) 1	\\	(3) 3	(4) 2	(1) 2	(1) 3
1 1/4-1 1/2	(12) 2	(9) 1	(3) 3	\\	(3) 0	(0) 0	(0) 0
1 1/2-1 3/4	(14) 2	(4) 1	(2) 2	(0) 3	\\	(1) 0	(1) 0

Juveniles

1/2-3/4	—	—	(0) 7	(0) 12	(0) 12	(0) 4	(0)
3/4-1	(1) 0	\\	(6) 8	(5) 5	(1) 3	(0) 0
1-1 1/4	(13) 0	(7) 0	\\	(2) 0	(1) 1	(0) 0
1 1/4-1 1/2	(5) 1	(7) 0	(0) 0	(0) 1	\\	(0) 0

<u>Note</u>: Number of Wadsworth users are in parentheses. Other numbers refer to Lovett users.

The relatively greater attractiveness of Wadsworth cannot be explained by the size of the library's bookstock since, in fact, Lovett has slightly more books than Wadsworth. The Lovett branch also has more floor area. The two branches are in about the same physical condition. Lovett was completely renovated and greatly enlarged in 1961, and Wadsworth was built in 1959. If penetration is to be explained, perhaps either a better measure of facility attractiveness is needed or else measures of neighborhood attractiveness should be included.

Overlap of the two market areas can be observed further by study of Table 34, which shows the percentage of library users in each distance cell who used Lovett Library for residential locations at various distances from the two libraries. Complete penetration occurred only in the locations 1½ to 1¾ miles from Lovett and 1¼ to 1½ miles from Wadsworth. All users from these locations, although they lived closer to the Wadsworth branch, used the Lovett branch. However, they number only three—a sample too small to be statistically reliable. The other cells where 100 percent of the users used Lovett are closer to Lovett and, therefore, would normally be expected to be in the Lovett market area. In most cells, a degree of overlap exists. Overlap is equal (with each library receiving 50 percent of the users) at residential locations which lie 1 to 1½ miles from Wadsworth and over 1 mile from Lovett. As would be expected, the percentage using a given library in general decreases with distance from the library.

The degree of overlap can be read more directly from Table 35 in which above the diagonal, where all cells refer to locations closer to Lovett, percentages refer to library users who use Lovett. Below the diagonal, where all cells refer to locations closer to Wadsworth, the percentages given are of library users who use Wadsworth. In this table, every entry would be 100 percent if there were no penetration.

Wadsworth and Lovett provide an example of a situation where both penetration and overlap exist. Wynnefield and Haddington provide an example of a situation where strong penetration occurs, but where overlap is not present. (See Table 36.) The existence of the main-line tracks of the Pennsylvania railroad between the two libraries (and about a mile from each) probably accounts for the lack of the typical fringe area of overlap. However, the Wynnefield branch draws a substantial number of users who live over one mile closer to the Haddington branch than to the Wynnefield branch. None of the people surveyed use Haddington while living closer to Wynnefield.

TABLE 34

Adult Library Users Who Use Lovett,
by Location of Residence
(in percent)

Miles from Residence to Lovett	1/2–3/4	Miles from Residence to Wadsworth				
		3/4-1	1-1 1/4	1 1/4-1 1/2	1 1/2-1 3/4	1 3/4-2
1/2–3/4	–	100	87	100	100	83
3/4-1	50	48	67	79	100	100
1-1 1/4	18	20	50	33	67	75
1 1/4-1 1/2	14	10	50	0	–	–
1 1/2-1 3/4	12.5	20	50	100	0	0

Note: Percent using Wadsworth = 100 – (% using Lovett)

TABLE 35

Adult Library Users Who Use Nearest Library,
by Location of Residence
(in percent)

Miles from Residence to Lovett	1/2– 3/4	Miles from Residence to Wadsworth				
		3/4-1	1-1 1/4	1 1/4-1 1/2	1 1/2-1 3/4	1 3/4-2
1/2–3/4	–	100	87	100	100	83
3/4-1	(50)	48 / 52	67	79	100	100
1-1 1/4	(82)	(80)	50	33	67	75
1 1/4-1 1/2	(86)	(90)	(50)	0	–	–
1 1/2-1 3/4	(87.5)	(80)	(50)	0	–	0

Note: Percent of Wadsworth users are in parentheses. Other numbers refer to Lovett users.

TABLE 36

Penetration of Haddington Market Area
by Wynnefield

Miles from Residence to Haddington	Miles from Residence to Wynnefield		
	2-2 1/4	2 1/4-2 1/2	2 1/2-2 3/4
3/4-1	7	7	
1-1 1/4		15	7
1 1/4-1 1/2		6	10
1 1/2-1 3/4		2	
1 3/4-2			
2-2 1/4			
2 1/4-2 1/2			

Note: Numbers refer to Wynnefield users. No Haddington users were found at the locations given in the table.

The relatively greater attraction of Wynnefield over Haddington is in accord with the bookstock of each: Wynnefield has 48,000 books while Haddington has only 24,000. This attraction may also be explainable on sociological grounds. All of the Wynnefield branch users who lived in the Haddington market area came from Overbrook Park. Both the Overbrook Park and Wynnefield neighborhoods are upper income and white, while the Haddington neighborhood is lower income and Negro.

Penetration of a Library into Market Areas of All Surrounding Libraries

From the preceding examples, it is not possible to judge whether a large proportion of users resides in areas characterized by penetration and overlap and, consequently, whether penetration and overlap are important considerations in the identification of market areas of libraries. This is because in each example interpenetration of one library has been studied only in relation to one other library, while a different degree of interpenetration may occur with other adjoining libraries.

All possible flows resulting from interpenetration are diagramed in Figure 40. In the preceding examples, flows such as those indicated by A and B have been identified. A complete identification of all flows would require that flows between all adjoining market areas be identified (flows A, B, C, D, E, F, G, and H). Since the survey was made of only seven libraries out of a total of forty, such complete identification is not possible. However it is possible to identify all flows resulting from persons who used a surveyed library although they lived closer to another library (flows B, D, F, and H). These represent penetration of the given library into the market areas of adjoining libraries. Data on such flows are summarized for four libraries

FIGURE 40

Possible Penetration Flows: a Given Library and Neighboring Libraries

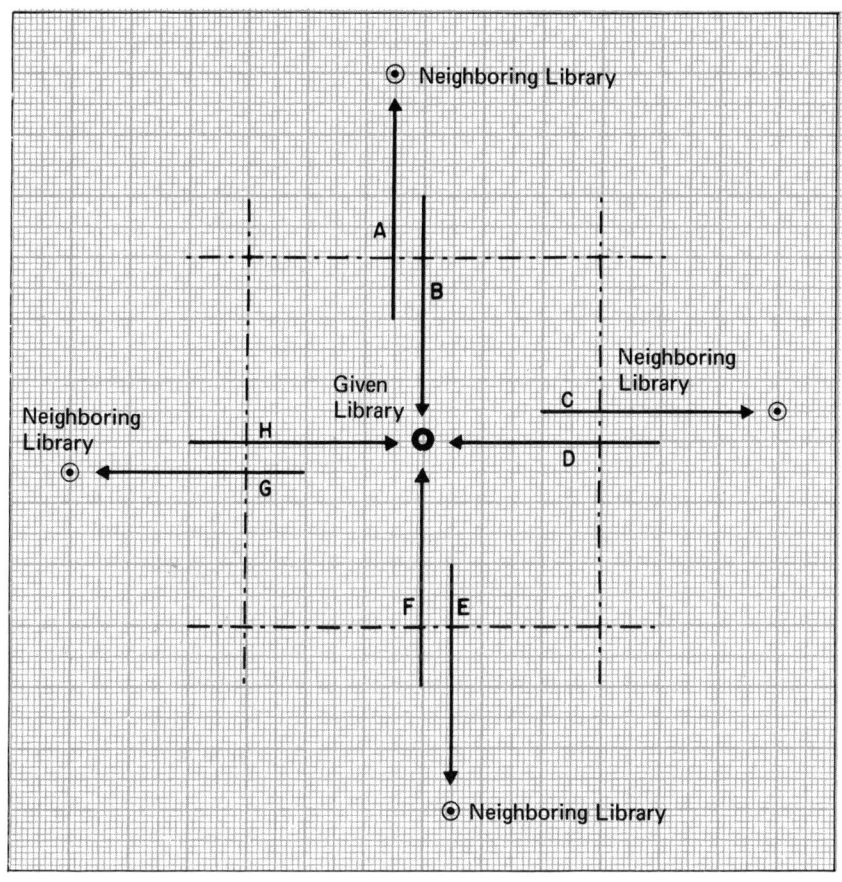

— · — · — Nominal Boundary of Service Area

in Table 37 and are given in detail in Table 38. In total, 9.4 percent of the users of the four libraries come from the natural market areas of adjoining libraries, though for individual libraries the percentage ranges from 1.8 percent to 15.2 percent.

For each of the four libraries, the percentage of adults coming from outside the library's natural market area is greater than the percentage of children coming from outside this area. This fact is consistent with the observation that, on the average, adults travel farther to get to the library than children do. Typically, the percentage for adults is about twice that for children.

It is not clear whether a person who resides at a given distance from two or more libraries is apt to use libraries more than a person who resides at the same given distance from only one library. Further analysis of the survey data might indicate slightly higher rates of use per capita in overlap areas, but the most important single spatial variable influencing use rate is still likely to be distance to the nearest library.

It is of some interest that the overlap is as small as it appears to be from the examples measured. Even in middle-class areas, whose population should be less sensitive to distance, users do not appear to bypass one library to go to another farther away. The overlap occurs mainly where it would be expected if the libraries were viewed by the users as being undifferentiated. That is, it occurs in the fringe areas between two libraries. The significant penetration of Haddington's market by the Wynnefield branch is not even as much as might be expected from the two to one difference in the size of the bookstocks of the two libraries. Therefore, further investigation of overlap can wait for later study, since its effect on system planning criteria does not appear significant in comparison with the effects of other aspects of the system.

Comparison of Market Area Penetration in Library Systems with Market Penetration in Other Service Systems

It is of interest to compare the degree of market penetration in the Philadelphia library system with that experienced in other service systems. The short-term general hospital system shares a number of characteristics with the library system but the choice of hospital is complicated by considerations of the doctor's affiliation with particular hospitals, the religious or other auspices of particular hospitals, and the variations in quality and price among hospitals.

One would expect all of these considerations to reduce the importance assigned to distance in determining the choice of a hospital. The data bear this out. For eight Cleveland hospitals measured (out of the total of twenty-four general hospitals), the percentage of users of a given hospital who live closer to another hospital ranges between 26.7 percent and 99 percent. (See Table 39.) Thus, for hospitals, penetration into market areas of adjoining units is much higher than for libraries.[12] The comparable percentages for selected libraries in Philadelphia was 1.8 percent to 15.2 percent.

TABLE 37

Penetration of Neighboring Service Areas by Selected Branch Libraries: Summary

	Branch Users Living Closer to Other Branches						Total Branch Users		
	Juveniles		Adults		Total				
	(number)	(percent)	(number)	(percent)	(number)	(percent)	Juveniles	Adults	Total
Wadsworth	38	13.3	75	16.4	113	15.2	286	458	744
Lovett	9	3.5	64	12.4	73	9.8	225	519	744
Columbia	13	4.7	13	7.6	26	5.8	278	171	449
Richmond	2	1.0	5	2.6	7	1.8	205	195	400
All above branches	62	6.3	157	11.7	219	9.4	994	1,343	2,337

TABLE 38

Penetration of Neighboring Service Areas by Selected Branch Libraries: Detail

	Juveniles	Adults
Wadsworth users living closer to:		
Lovett	14	30
West Oak Lane	28	55
Chestnut Hill	0	3
Total living closer to surrounding branches[a]	38	75
(Percent of total Wadsworth users)	(13.3)	(16.4)
Total Wadsworth users	286	458
Lovett users living closer to:		
Wadsworth	4	29
Chesnut Hill	2	5
West Oak Lane	3	21
Germantown	4	29
Total living closer to surrounding branches[a]	9	64
(Percent of total Lovett users)	(3.5)	(12.4)
Total Lovett users	255	519
Columbia users living closer to:		
Widener	13	12
Community	0	0
Main Library	0	0
Total living closer to surrounding branches[a]	13	13
(Percent of total Columbia users)	(4.7)	(7.6)
Total Columbia users	278	171
Richmond users living closer to:		
Kensington	0	3
McPherson	2	4
Frankford	0	0
Total living closer to surrounding branches[a]	2	5
(Percent of total Richmond users)	(0.97)	(2.6)
Total Columbia users	205	195

[a]The total is sometimes smaller than the sum of individual surrounding branches, since a user living closer to two surrounding branches would be listed separately for each individual branch, but would be counted only once in the total.

TABLE 39

Penetration of Neighboring Natural Market Areas by Selected Hospitals in the Cleveland Metropolitan Area[a]

Hospital	In-Patients Closer to Given Hospital (number)	(percent)	In-Patients Closer to Other Hospitals (number)	(percent)	Total (number)	(percent)	Location[b]	Facilities in Hospital[c] (number)
Bedford	52	73.3	19	26.7	71	100	Edge	8
Berea Community	181	61.5	114	38.5	295	100	Edge	18
Euclid-Glenville	242	56.8	184	43.2	426	100	Edge	20
Evangelical Deaconess	318	49.5	313	50.4	631	100	Suburban	22
Fair View Park	194	29.8	458	70.2	652	100	Suburban	23
Forest Hill Obstetrical	59	21.8	220	78.2	279	100	Suburban	22
Bayview	8	17.0	38	83.0	46	100	Edge	no answer
Doctor's	1	1.0	159	99.0	160	100	Suburban	20

[a] Computed from maps of residence of obstetrical patients in Citizens Hospital Study Committee, Hospitals and Their Use in Northeast Ohio (Cleveland, 1961), pt. 11.
[b] "Edge" refers to the edge of the metropolitan area. "Suburban" refers to a suburban location.
[c] From "Services Available," Hospitals, Journal of the American Hospital Association (Guide Issue, 1962). Facilities include, for example, clinical laboratory, pathology laboratory, X-ray therapy, intensive care unit, and premature nursery.

NOTES

1. Nominal service areas refer to areas defined by librarians. See Chapter 4.

2. The minimum value of r for significance at the 0.05 level is 0.7067.

3. Rate of use by adults is calculated for each of the distance "rings," defined in chapter 5, by dividing the number of adult users residing in each ring by the estimated adult population in that ring. Similar calculations were made for persons fourteen to eighteen years old and persons under fourteen years old. See Chapter 6 for the method of estimating population in each distance ring.

4. The age classification used in this chapter is "under fourteen, fourteen to eighteen, and over eighteen" to correspond to data on resident population available from the United States Census Bureau.

5. One alternative measure might be the minimal use radius: that distance beyond which use would have fallen below some acceptable absolute standard. Typically, the standard would be an absolute one applicable to all residents regardless of their desire for library service. It would be based on some judgment of the minimal level of library service that should be available to each person in the system's service area. Such a minimal service radius would vary over a very large range.

For a discussion of other approaches to service area measurement, see Jerry B. Schneider, "The Spatial Structure of the Medical Care Process," RSRI Paper, No. 14, and H. D. Cherniack and Jerry B. Schneider, "A New Approach to the Delineation of Hospital Service Areas," RSRI Discussion Paper, No. 16.

6. Variation would be much greater for the alternative "radius at the minimum acceptable level," which is defined in note 5, above. For example, assume the minimal acceptable use level to be that base level use rate found in the neighborhood of the library with the lowest base use level. For our sample, that would be 1.54 users per 1,000 residents found within $\frac{1}{4}$ mile of the Columbia branch. The minimal service radius for the same level of service for Wynnefield

The Effects of Location on Library Use

would be between 1¾ and 2 miles—that is, on the order of eight times as far.

7. The correlation between the number of users in the two-day sample and the size of the bookstock was 0.901.

8. For a discussion of models of distance decay and their underlying rationale, see G. A. P. Carrothers, "An Historical Review of Gravity and Potential Concepts of Human Interaction," *Journal of the American Institute of Planners* 22:94–102, and Gunnar Olsson, *Distance and Human Interaction,* Bibliography Series No. 2 (Philadelphia: RSRI, 1965).

9. Failure to observe the expected relations may, of course, be the result of an inaccurate concept and measurement of "commercial area." As noted above, measurement was made of the acreage of land in commercial use. This included areas used for retail sales and services alone or with residential space above the first floor, offices, and parking. A different definition or a weighting according to intensity of use would lead to different commercial indexes, which might result in improved correlations. A different weighting of distance also would change the indexes. The indexes presented were formulated with distance squared. If distance were cubed, the relative contribution of the most distant commercial locations would be reduced. If it were at the first power, their relative contribution to the index would be increased.

10. Philadelphia City Planning Commission, *Population Estimate as of July 1, 1964* (Philadelphia, 1966), for planning analysis sections and sub-sections of Philadelphia.

11. In this chapter, adults are defined as persons fourteen years old and over and children or juveniles as persons under fourteen years of age.

12. The degree of penetration is so different for the libraries and hospitals studied that this can be concluded despite the fact that the libraries and hospitals were selected arbitrarily and probably did not represent the full range of variation.

7

CONCLUSIONS AND IMPLICATIONS FOR LIBRARY SYSTEM PLANNING

SUMMARY OF FINDINGS

This study has aimed at providing an improved basis for planning a system of branch libraries and for programming additional branches or other improvements to an existing system. A number of conclusions have been reached from the analysis of the system of the Free Library of Philadelphia, and these conclusions may turn out to be valid for other library systems.

1. The most important factor determining the amount of use made of a library is the socioeconomic level of the residents in its service area.

2. The bookstock appears to be the next most important factor. Location near a school or in a shopping center is a less important factor.

3. The use rate (per 1,000 residents in a given age group) by juveniles and young adults is much higher than by adults (in the order of five to ten times as high in middle- and upper-

Conclusions and Implications 151

class areas and of the order of twenty times as high in lower-class areas).

4. The radius of the market area of a library (defined as the area from which 80 percent of the users of the library come) generally ranges between 0.4 miles and 1.2 miles for children, between 0.6 miles and 1.5 miles for teen-agers, and between 0.5 and 1.85 miles for adults. The radius is shortest for libraries in areas of low socioeconomic status. The larger radii all occur in areas of higher socioeconomic status. One Philadelphia branch library in a high status area, for example, has a market area radius of over 2 miles for both teen-agers and adults.

5. The base level use rate (the number of visits per 1,000 residents within $\frac{1}{4}$ mile of the library, where distance does not inhibit use) is higher in middle- and upper-class areas than it is in areas of low socioeconomic status. However, the variation in use rate level among children from areas of different socioeconomic class is much smaller than among adults. The low base level use rate in low-income areas does not seem to be caused directly by the small size of the bookstock, since the number of borrowings per book in such areas is roughly one-half that in high-income areas. However, since the size of the bookstock in libraries in low-income areas is on the order of one-half that of libraries in high-income areas, part of the explanation of the low borrowing rate may be the lack of selection (although all of the surveyed libraries had over 20,000 books each). Another may be that the selection of books available in lower-income areas may not be well matched to the tastes, interests, and reading abilities of the public served. The establishment of such conclusions, however, would require additional research.

6. Effective service radius is longest for libraries in areas of high socioeconomic status and shortest for libraries in areas of low status. The effective service radius is defined in this study

as the distance out to the point where the use rate falls to 10 percent of the base level use rate. Thus it is the distance beyond which at least 90 percent of potential users are deterred from using that library. Use rate by adults, however, falls off faster in areas of high social status and slower in areas of low social status. It is only because base level use rates are so high in high status areas that effective service radii are longer for libraries in such areas than for libraries in areas of lower socioeconomic status.

7. Some overlap of market areas exists. The percentage of users of a given branch who actually live closer to another branch ranges between 1.8 percent and 15.2 percent for the four branches that were measured. This relatively small degree of overlap indicates that library users consider all branches to be essentially equivalent and, therefore, tend to go to the nearest one.

OBJECTIVES OF A SYSTEM PLAN

These, and other more detailed findings, should be of use to the planner of a library system. However, before any such findings can be put to use in planning, it is necessary to determine the objective of the plan being prepared. Since we do not know how library use affects public welfare in the long run, we concentrate here on short-run objectives. Even the specification of short-run objectives involves problems, which are due, in part, to the interdependent nature of all public goals as discussed in chapter 2. In addition, as with many other public services, the outputs of a library system are varied, subtle, and difficult to measure.

For these reasons, two alternative simple objectives, both of which have been suggested by library administrators and public

Conclusions and Implications   153

planning agencies, will be examined here. These alternatives are to maximize library service for the system as a whole or to equalize service in all parts of the total service area of the system. In this context, service is defined in terms of the use made of the services rather than of the amount of services offered.

If the objective is to maximize service for the system as a whole, the obvious policy for achieving this objective is to place libraries closer together in middle- and upper-income areas. These areas exhibit the highest use rates by far, and, in addition, their users are very sensitive to distance. Although policies for achieving such an objective are relatively easy to set, the objective is questionable for a public agency. In fact, it could be argued that such an objective could be achieved more efficiently and more suitably by a private company.

The fact that the library system is public implies that its objective is to provide service to the public as a whole. This is because the system provides public benefits which are long-term and widespread and therefore would not accrue to a private library entrepreneur as profits. Lacking a return on such external economies of a library system, a private entrepreneur would have to price library services at a level that would prohibit their use by lower-income persons. The library system, therefore, is public because it is in the public interest to provide equal opportunity for library service just as with educational and other services.

The objective of planning a single library system to serve the entire public, then, must be in some sense to equalize service throughout the entire area served. We have defined service as the amount of service used, but this is affected not only by the amount of service supplied, but also by the amount of service demanded. In addition, use rate declines with distance from library. Therefore, it is conceptually difficult, and practically impossible, to design a library system so that the use rate everywhere would be equal.

One possible planning approach is to set up market radius standards that describe the average or maximum distance people will travel to a library. These could be based on observations of the size of actual market areas. For example, the survey has shown that in lower-status areas 80 percent of all library users live within $\frac{1}{2}$ mile of the library they use, and in upper-class areas 80 percent of all users live within $1\frac{1}{2}$ miles. Therefore, market radius standards of $\frac{1}{2}$ and $1\frac{1}{2}$ miles might be used for such areas. However, market radius standards of this sort do not imply equality of service in any sense.

A more suitable approach might be to determine a minimum acceptable use rate and to plan the system so that such a use rate could be expected in each residential area. At this point in library system research, however, it would be impossible to determine a minimum use rate that would be acceptable in an absolute sense. We do not have any idea, for example, of the relationship between library use rate and success in school and employment or of the relationship between library accessibility and the desirability of a residential neighborhood.

Minimum acceptable use rates might be set in relation to base level use rates. The base level use rate is the rate of use made of a "free" good—a good with virtually no money cost or travel cost—and, therefore, is an approximation of unrestricted demand for that good. The minimum acceptable use rate might be defined as some percentage of that unrestricted use rate. Earlier, $\frac{1}{10}$ of the base level use rate was implied to be acceptable and was the basis for determining the effective service radius. However, a higher acceptable minimum might be set.

ANALYSIS OF ALTERNATIVE LIBRARY SYSTEMS

A complete analytic scheme for analyzing alternative library systems will not be presented here.[1] However, it is instructive to examine some of the implications of our findings for the development of such a framework.

Use rates of hypothetical library systems can be diagramed as in Figure 41. As diagramed, base level use rate depends entirely upon the social characteristics of the residents, although it is certain that over some range the size of bookstock influences use rate. Again hypothetically, an effective service radius is assumed to be determined entirely by size of bookstock. Use rate is assumed to fall off linearly with distance. All these assumptions are generally consistent with the relationships developed previously, although more precise relationships might be identified after a more thorough analysis.

Perfect library service might be defined as the service level that would result in base level use everywhere. Since use rate declines with distance, perfect library service is virtually unattainable.

The actual total system use is represented by the shaded area in Figure 41, and the total system use level can be conceived of as the percentage of the total rectangle represented by the shaded area. It is evident that the service level is considerably higher in the one-library system of a large bookstock library than in the system consisting of one small bookstock library (Figure 41).

System use level can be increased by making libraries more accessible. The addition of more libraries is an obvious way to do this.[2] In Figure 41 B, two libraries have been added to each system. It is evident that the system of large bookstock libraries

FIGURE 41

Service Levels of Simple Hypothetical Library Systems

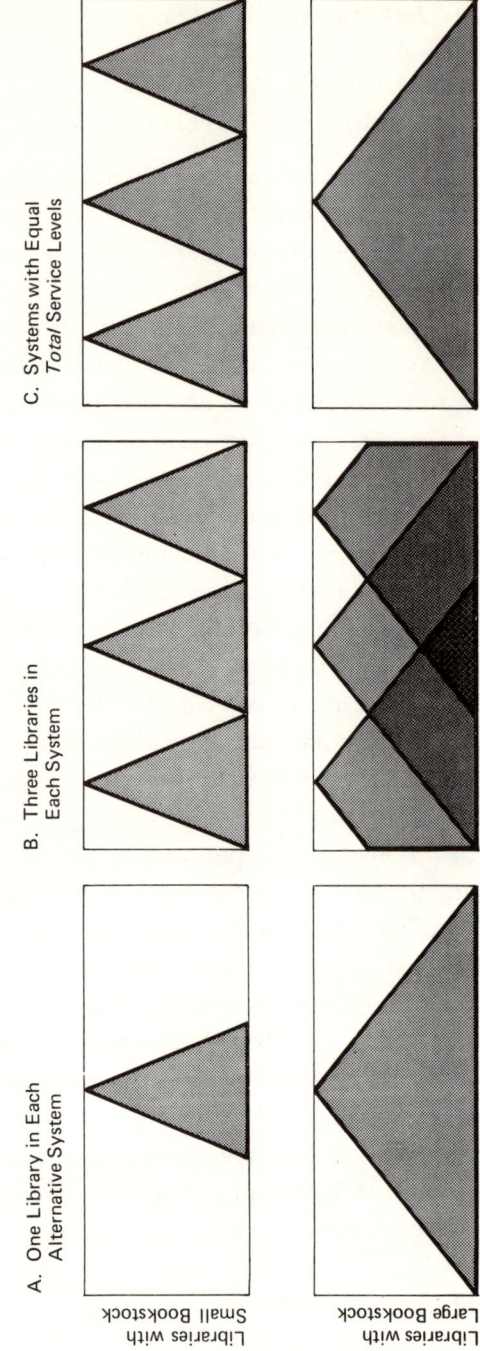

A. One Library in Each Alternative System

B. Three Libraries in Each System

C. Systems with Equal *Total* Service Levels

Libraries with Small Bookstock

Libraries with Large Bookstock

NOTE: These diagrams based on assumptions that
1) Residents at uniform density and all of one socioeconomic level
2) Base level use rate depends entirely upon socioeconomic level of residents
3) Radius of effective service increases with size of bookstock

Conclusions and Implications

still provides the higher level of service. However, it appears that the relative gain of the large bookstock system is smaller than that achieved by the small bookstock system. In the large bookstock system, the addition of new branches leads to extensive overlap of service area, while in the small bookstock system new branches serve people who were previously outside effective service areas.

It is possible, however, that the accessibility of more than one library to residents in areas of overlap would result in higher service levels than those diagramed. For example, a resident of such an area would be able to choose between the original library and a second library which is located a little farther from his home. In fact, the second library might prove to be the more convenient for him because it might be located near where he shops or on the way to or near his workplace. Estimation of the effect of additional libraries on the use rate in overlap areas has not been possible in this study, but is a problem worthy of future research.

Measurement of system service level by the proportion of the perfect service rectangle which is shaded can be misleading. This is particularly evident in Figure 41 C, where a system consisting of three small bookstock libraries is compared with a system consisting of one large bookstock library. Such a measurement of system service level does not enable one to distinguish between these two systems. For each of them, actual system service level is 50 percent of the perfect system service level.

The pattern of service levels, however, is quite different in the two systems. Persons living near the edges of the total service area fare far better with the three-library system than with the one-library system. If residents cannot all be considered as having an equal need for library service, a measure of library system service level would be adequate only if it identified service with specific groups of people or to specific locations.

If it is recognized that the socioeconomic level of residents is different in different parts of the metropolitan area, the simple diagrams of Figure 41 no longer suffice. Instead, for branch libraries of the same size and quality, base level use rate may be diagramed as proportional to the socioeconomic level of residents, as in Figure 42.

In such a diagram that is more realistic than that of Figure 41, criteria for equitable spacing of libraries are difficult to set. One possibility is a criterion that states that libraries should be located so as to provide every residential block with some absolute minimum level of library service, as diagramed in Figure 42 A. Such a uniform criterion, however, is not related to the amount of library service desired by each socioeconomic group. As a result, service provided at the edge of service areas would be high relative to the demand for low-income areas and relatively low for higher status areas.

Alternatively, the minimum service level permitted might be defined as the level that occurs at the effective service radius of each library. The object of such a criterion, diagramed in Figure 42 B, would be to provide equal service relative to demand and, therefore, to have equally satisfied residents along the edges of all service areas. With such a criterion, the absolute level of service is lower at the effective service radius of libraries in low-income areas than of libraries in high-income areas.[3]

The extreme variation found in base level use rate in the Philadelphia system leads to a practical problem. If the minimum acceptable use level were 10 percent of the base level use rate, the adult base level use rate at a library in an area like that of the Columbia branch would be smaller than the rate at the effective service radius in areas of higher socioeconomic status such

FIGURE 42

Alternate Criteria for Minimum Acceptable Service Levels for Hypothetical Library Systems

A. Absolute Minimum Levels

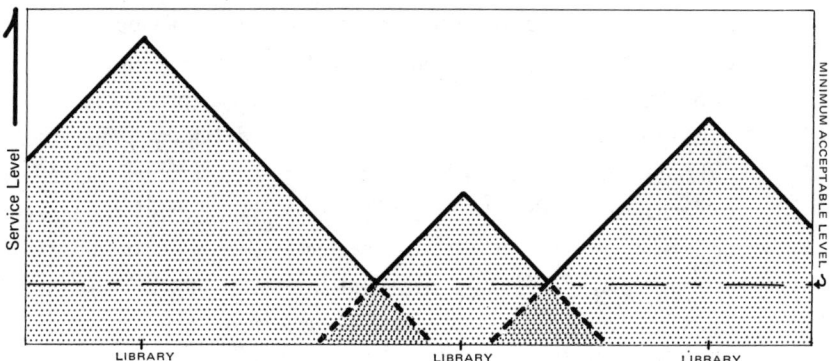

B. Levels at Effective Service Radii
   (assume 20 percent of Base Level Use Rate)

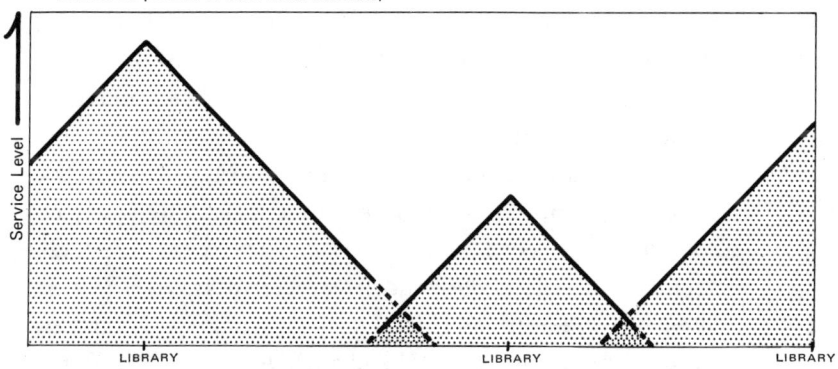

NOTE: In these diagrams, residents near each library are assumed to be of different socioeconomic levels. Base level use rate is assumed to depend entirely on socioeconomic level of residents.

as Frankford, Lovett, Wadsworth, and Wynnefield. If such areas were adjacent, it would not be possible to design a library system without major discontinuities in service levels. Even if residents were located so that gradation in social level was gradual, it might still be impossible to design a system without significant discontinuities in service level.

Our data indicate that even if use rate were equalized relative to demand, the differential between different areas or groups of residents would be so great that the result could not be considered satisfactory from a social point of view. The obvious solution is to raise base level use rate in lower-class areas. Undoubtedly this can be done through well-devised library programs, although our limited analysis indicates that base level use rate is determined primarily by the socioeconomic class of residents and therefore may not be easily affected by changes in the library system. Increases in bookstock and improvements in other aspects of the attractiveness of the library must have some effect upon base level use, although this fact cannot be deduced from our data. Measurement of the suitability of the bookstock and of special programs designed for the cultural needs of the residents was not possible in this study, but it, too, could be expected to have some effect on base level use rate.

An optimum library system plan could not be formulated without also exploring the results of variation in the size and spacing of libraries. Because of the effect of size on the effective service radius, these two dimensions of a system are closely interrelated in the way in which they influence system use level. So long as the effects of service area overlap are minor, these additional considerations present practical complexity, but few conceptual problems. Our data and analysis do not permit us to predict results when spacing is made so close that overlap becomes a major problem. The analytic model could be simplified

Conclusions and Implications

considerably by not allowing such close spacing and by disregarding the effects of overlap. Finally, in designing an optimal system, it would seem advisable to seek beyond the limited data presented and to determine the effects which bookstock size and composition must logically have upon base level use rate.

Systematic exploration of possible library sizes and geographic configurations, however, is but one side of the planning problem. The other side is the cost of each of the possible systems. Normally the problem posed is either to design the cheapest system to achieve a given system service level or to design the system providing the highest possible service level for a given cost. Only when cost is considered can one evaluate the trade-off between larger and more efficient libraries and a greater number of libraries more closely spaced.

MAJOR QUESTIONS FOR FUTURE RESEARCH

This study has been, admittedly, exploratory, for, as was noted at the start of this report, very few analytic studies of library systems exist. The results, therefore, are not definitive. In fact, among the more important results may be suggestions for future research. Several of the prominent suggestions are listed here.

1. Does use rate per 1,000 residents *in general* fall faster with distance for people in higher occupational levels? Our data suggest that this may be true—a finding at variance with findings of other studies concerning travel habits and social status. If it is true, an adequate explanation of this behavior pattern would have to be sought, perhaps by exploring the reasons suggested in the text.

2. To what extent is accessibility to more than one library likely to increase the amount a person uses a library?

3. Over what range does an increase in bookstock cause an increase in base level use rate? What other methods of increasing base level use rate are possible? Answers to these questions are most important in the attempt to improve service to low-income areas.

4. Does increase in bookstock cause an increase in effective service radius, or is it simply that neighborhoods of high occupational level demand well-stocked libraries, get them, and use them? Causality is always most difficult to determine, yet it is the one aspect of which the system planner would like to be assured.

5. The preceding questions refer to specific library system objectives. Further study of effects on broader community objectives should also be carried out.

6. What is the effect of library use on school performance, future earnings, etc.?

7. What is the effect of a good library upon residential location decisions? Do the quality and location of the library, in combination with other public facilities, constitute a significant factor affecting neighborhood desirability?

The authors cannot claim that the results of this study have been conclusive. In particular, the findings fail to point definitively to system policies that might lead to major increase in library use in lower income areas. The items of suggested future research that bear on this problem should be given highest priority. Nevertheless, we feel that our findings are of sufficient interest to warrant additional research of this kind. It is clear that the understanding of public service systems necessary to effective planning for such systems is insufficient not only for libraries but for most other public facilities. A vastly increased base of knowledge about such systems is necessary for the rational solution of urban problems.

NOTES

1. A simple heuristic model is presented by Michael B. Teitz, *Toward a Theory of Public Facility Location,* Working Paper No. 67 (Berkeley: Center for Planning and Development Research, Institute of Urban and Regional Development, University of California, Berkeley, 1967). In his model, spatial distribution is not a subject of analysis.

2. Another way is to make libraries more accessible by improving transportation to them. Since the focus of this study is upon policies that libraries can put into effect, this alternative will not be pursued here. Yet another way is to make libraries more accessible by bringing them to the people—by making more extensive use of mobile libraries.

3. A problem occurs on the boundary between the service areas of two libraries that are located in areas of different socioeconomic levels: a resident of an area of service overlap is at the limit of effective service with reference to one library, but is above that minimum in relationship to the other library. Whether he is at or above the minimum acceptable level depends upon which population group he is similar to: the group living around the first library or that living around the second library. The problem of how to model the continuous changes in characteristics of actual population is raised here. This problem would make the modeling of an actual system very complex.

INDEX

Accessibility, 3, 52-55, 155, 161;
  to schools, 40, 53-57, 64, 96,
  131-134; to commercial areas,
  40, 50-52, 57, 61, 64, 96, 131,
  132, 133, 134
Adjoining county, users from, 98,
  99, 129
Adult users, 40, 42, 43, 52, 53,
  56, 67, 69, 78, 82, 99, 102,
  105-108, 110, 114, 115, 121-
  124, 129, 131, 133, 150, 151
Age of library users, 67, 71
Assistance from staff, 74, 75

Base level use rate, 116, 117-119,
  121, 122, 123, 129, 130, 131,
  133, 134, 151, 154, 158, 160,
  162
Bookstock, 23, 24, 30, 40, 45,
  46, 47, 64, 83, 103, 107, 117,
  118, 119, 122, 129, 130, 133,
  134, 139, 142, 150, 151, 155,
  160, 162
  pressure on, 80

Capital programs, 5
Capital value of library, 48, 49
Characteristics of libraries in
  survey, 63
Children's librarian, 48, 49
Circulation, 21, 23, 32-37, 45,
  48, 50, 64, 103, 106
  circulation per capita, 39, 40,
  42-57
Constraints, 7, 9
Cost of providing library service,
  161
Cost of using library service, 3,
  154
Crowdedness, 83, 131, 133

Decline in use rate with distance,
  116, 118, 119, 128, 130
Demand for library service, 26,
  44, 80, 130, 153, 154
Distance from home to library,
  84ff, 112-115, 118, 134, 141,
  154, 155

165

Distance to next nearest library, 40, 64, 103, 108
Duluth Public Library system, 110, 118

Educational level of residents in service area, 42, 61
Effective service radius, *116,* 118, 119, 121, 124, 126, 129-131, 134, 151, 158
Equalization of service, 153ff

Floor space, 40, 64, 134
Future research, suggestions for, 161, 162

Goals, community, 4, 5, 9, 15, 16, 153, 162
Goals, functional, 4, 5, 9, 152, 153, 162
  See also Objectives of library system
Goals, general, 7, 9, 152

Hospital systems, 145, 147

Income of residents in service area, 40, 42, 61, 128, 131, 133, 158

Juvenile & adult users, relationship between, 55-57, 82, 102
Juvenile users, 24, 40, 42, 44, 53, 56, 67, 78, 79, 82, 99, 102, 105-108, 110, 112, 113, 115, 117, 119, 121-124, 129, 131, 133, 150, 151

Library users, characteristics of, 62-73; age, 67; sex, 67, 70, 71; occupation, 70-72
Library visit, purposes of, 72-74
Location of library, 39, 50-55
  See also Accessibility to commercial areas; Accessibility to schools; Distance to next nearest library
Low-income areas, characteristics of users and use, 76, 80, 82
Low-income areas, service to, 70, 128, 151, 153, 160, 162

Market area radius, 98, 101-108, 118, 126, 129, 134, 151, 154
Market areas, 3, 103, 109
Multistop trips to library, 84, 85, 96-98, 127, 134, 135

Noise, 55, 82
Nominal service area, 38, 103

Objectives of library system, 11-15
Occupations of adult library users, 70, 73, 118
Occupations of residents of service area, 39-46, 48, 49, 52, 54, 61, 64, 102, 105, 117, 119, 123, 124, 129, 131, 133, 134
Open-shelf material, 74
Operating costs, 24
Operating expenses, 23, 30
Other libraries, use of, 76-79
Output of a library, 20-23, 30, 39, 42; determinants of out-

Index

put, 22-26; demand vs. supply as determinant of output, 26, 44, 80, 130
Overlap of service areas, 77, 103, 130, 136ff, 140, 152, 157, 160 See also Penetration

Parking space, 51, 83
Penetration of service or market areas, 136-146, 157, 159
Philadelphia Free Library system, 21, 28, 29, 30, 32-37, 40, 61, 63
Policies, 8-11
Population estimates, 135
Population subgroups, 10
Professional services, 21, 23, 25, 39, 40, 82
Public facility programming, 4
Public facility systems, 4, 145

Quality of library, 45-50, 160
Questionnaire, 66, 68

Regional libraries, 28, 77
Registration, 21, 30, 40
Residents in service area, characteristics of and effect on library output, 39-45, 109, 131

Satisfaction of user, 79, 81

Seating space, 83
Services, use of in library, 74, 75; open-shelf materials, 74-75; book borrowing, 74, 75, 77; seek assistance from staff, 74, 75, 77
Sex of library users, 67, 70, 72
Socioeconomic status, 39, 45, 48, 61, 102, 117, 119, 128, 129, 131, 133, 151, 152, 158, 160
System planning, 3, 129, 130, 134-137, 150-162
System service level, 156, 157; discontinuities in, 160; See also Use, total system

Transit, availability of, 97, 128
Transportation to libraries, means of, 97, 98
Travel to the library, 84, 96, 97

Use, total system, 155; See System service level
Use rate, 109-116, 155, 161; minimum acceptable, 154, 158
Users of branch libraries, number of, 89-95, 115; number per 1,000 population, 112-115, 118

Variety of choice of branch, 130

About the Authors

Robert E. Coughlin is Vice President and Treasurer of the Regional Science Research Institute in Philadelphia. He received his Master in City Planning from the Massachusetts Institute of Technology and his Ph.D. from the University of Pennsylvania. Dr. Coughlin is co-author, with Walter Isard, of *Municipal Costs and Revenues Resulting from Community Growth* (1957). Among his published articles are several on public facility system planning and programming, and on the interrelationships between urbanization and the natural environment, as well as on other aspects of city and regional planning.

Françoise Taïeb is Research Associate at the Center for Studies in City Development (CERAU) in Paris. She has worked previously as Research Associate at the Center for Research and Documentation for Consumer Industry (CREDOC) in France and at the Regional Science Research Institute in Philadelphia. Mrs. Taïeb studied at Paris University, where she was awarded Licence en Sciences Mathèmatiques, Diplome de l'Institute de Statistiques.

Benjamin H. Stevens is President of the Regional Science Research Institute. A Professor in the Regional Science Department at the University of Pennsylvania, he is presently coordinator for Urban Regional and Environmental Studies at that university. He earned his Master in City Planning and Ph.D. in city and regional planning at the Massachusetts Institute of Technology. Dr. Stevens has written numerous articles on the subject of urban and regional planning and is co-author, with Carolyn A. Brackett, of *Industrial Location: A Review and Annotated Bibliography of Theoretical, Empirical and Case Studies* (1967).

Urban Analysis for Branch Library System Planning was composed in linotype Garamond with Garamond Bold display by Pyramid Composition Company, Inc., New York, New York. The entire book was printed by offset lithography by Litho Crafters, Inc., Ann Arbor, Michigan.

Z
686
C67

OCT 26 1972